Chasing the Heretics

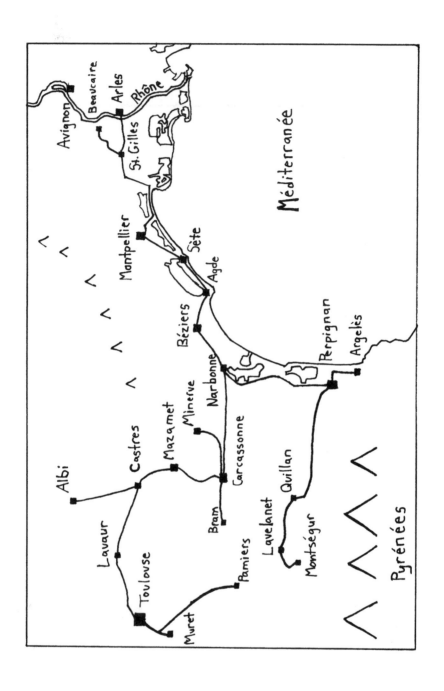

Chasing the Heretics

A Modern Journey through the Medieval Languedoc

RION KLAWINSKI

Hungry Mind Press

SAINT PAUL, MINNESOTA

Published by Hungry Mind Press
1648 Grand Avenue
Saint Paul, MN 55105

ISBN: 1-886913-27-7
Library of Congress Catalog Number: 99-71512

10 9 8 7 6 5 4 3 2 1
First Hungry Mind Press Printing 1999

Book design by Wendy Holdman
Dustjacket design by Valerie Brewster
Map design by Greg Fitz
Typesetting by Stanton Publication Services

Printed in the United States of America

This book is dedicated to
my Mom and Dad
and to
Susan

Contents

Acknowledgments

I would like to thank Pearl Kilbride of Hungry Mind Press for all her work and support, Susan Day and Mary Byers for their keen comments and skilled editing, and my friend and mentor, Enid Powell, for her help when this book was a fledgling.

Chasing the Heretics

The Murder at the Rhône

THE D'ARLATAN HOTEL HIDES AWAY IN THE MAZE OF NARROW
streets that make up the medieval quarter of Arles in southern
France. Before being converted into a hotel in the early 1900s, the
D'Arlatan boasted of having been the ancestral home of the dukes
of Arlatan since the thirteenth century, and the place works hard
to maintain a medieval illusion. The public rooms consist of several small salons. Armor hangs on the dark wooden walls next to a
pair of huge crossed swords. One blade sports a large dent in its
middle, suggesting that it was once used for more than decoration.

Modern technology is kept purposely discreet. The desk clerk's
computer terminal, its cold, mechanical green glow reflected in his
eyeglasses, is concealed behind a rough-hewn panel; the lobby
telephone is hidden in a small wooden box with weathered brass
hinges, the fax machine and switchboard are tucked away in a rear
office. Electric lights mounted on the walls and disguised as
torches break the deliberate dimness with small pools of light.

I preferred one salon in particular, with an uneven stone floor, a
blackened hearth high as my shoulder occupying an entire wall,
and heavy chairs with brocaded seats and high wooden backs. The
ceiling was rough and white and crisscrossed by scarred wooden
beams. I sank down into one of the chairs, temporarily satisfied to
survey the medieval trappings.

The first days of a journey have always liberated me. Daily routine dims to unimportant memory. Energy flows from the beckoning roads. Senses are primed for new experience. No vital travel connections have been missed and urgency is not in the forecast. A walk down a forgotten country road is the equal of a transcontinental train ride in adventure.

But this time my body and mind were tired. Fatigue had prematurely set in on the long, cramped transatlantic flight from Chicago to Paris. I sat next to an arrhythmic snorer who fell asleep after takeoff and stayed that way until we were over the English Channel. His noises robbed me of the chance to read, rest, or just sit peacefully in the engines' drone.

Mostly, though, I was jealous of his oblivion. My fatigue grew during the eight-hundred-kilometer drive from Charles de Gaulle airport, where I picked up my little blue Peugeot, through the hinterlands of Paris and rolling Burgundy, over the hump of the Massif Central, then along the Rhône River valley south of Lyon to my hotel on the outskirts of Arles.

French truck drivers were angry at Spanish truck drivers who were bringing produce into France from Spain over the Pyrenees, and they seemed to be taking it out on the rest of us. When not blocking toll booths they drove like men possessed by angry devils, tailgating, changing lanes without signals, all at 130 kilometers per hour. I was also unable to shake my jet lag, curse of the late twentieth century, and had difficulty adjusting to the time difference, sleeping in fits of two to three hours for the first several days.

All good reasons to stay locked in the comfortable arms of the D'Arlatan salon and its thirteenth-century fakery. But the thirteenth century that I had come to Arles to search out contained a murder most foul—an extraordinary murder, even for those violent times, committed in the dawn hours of a January morning in the long-ago year of 1208; a murder whose consequences mark the face of southern France to this day; a murder whose traces weren't to be found in the salons of the D'Arlatan.

On the morning of 14 January 1208, Peter of Castelnau, Cistercian monk and legate of Pope Innocent III to the Languedoc region of southern France, was camped on the west bank of the Rhône River, a little to the north of the ramparts of thirteenth-century Arles, preparing to cross. The river marked the border between the Languedoc and Provence, then a part of the Holy Roman Empire. The day before, Peter, with his entourage, had quickly departed the Abbey of St-Gilles, ten miles to the west of the main river on the banks of its offshoot, the Petit Rhône, after reluctantly terminating his long, unsuccessful, eventually acrimonious parley with the most powerful noble in the Languedoc, Raymond VI, the count of Toulouse.

The year before, Peter had excommunicated Raymond because of the count's refusal to act against the Cathars, a religious sect decreed heretical by the Church of Rome. Over the past two hundred years, the sect had spread throughout the Languedoc and taken firm root. The count paid elaborate lip service to Peter in order to end his excommunication, but he avoided making any firm promises to root out the Cathars, who freely practiced their faith on the lands the count controlled. Unable to extract a firm commitment from Raymond to perform what the church believed was the count's duty as both a Christian and a nobleman, Peter broke off the talks and departed the abbey. He would have no good news to report to the pope.

Peter never made his report. Before he could cross the Rhône, a lone horseman wielding a lance galloped into his camp. Riding up to Peter he pierced the legate in the back, killing him instantly. In the confusion that followed, the horseman escaped in the direction of Beaucaire, a nearby town friendly to the count of Toulouse. A number of men in Peter's camp identified the murderer as a member of Raymond's entourage at the abbey.

News of the murder and the alleged perpetrator reached Rome. Although evidence was scant that Peter's murder was actually instigated by Raymond VI, it was sufficient for Pope Innocent III, a man afraid of neither quick judgment nor fast action. He immediately fixed the responsibility for Peter's death on Raymond.

Raymond VI of Toulouse had not only refused to battle the Cathars but was now implicated in the heinous murder of a papal legate. He, along with the whole of the Languedoc, would have to suffer the terrible consequences. The pope was forced to seek defenders of the faith beyond the borders of the Languedoc to eradicate the heresy that threatened the very foundations of Mother Church. Innocent wrote a fiery letter to the Cistercian abbeys in the north of France calling upon the brothers of Peter of Castelnau to preach a crusade against the Cathar heretics in the Languedoc. By July of the following year, a great crusader army was massed at Lyon, preparing to march into the Languedoc and make war in the name of God.

I believed I would be able to view the scene of the murder from the medieval ramparts that still stand to the north of the D'Arlatan. The ramparts, more than twenty feet high, once encircled the entire medieval quarter, but over the centuries most of their length had been engulfed by the ever-spreading town. Now only one small section along the Rhône, perhaps one hundred feet long, was all that remained of them. A short distance upstream, I calculated, at the point where the Rhône divides, marked the spot of the murder. But I was still sitting in the salon, needing an impetus to visit the site. It was provided by a beautiful Japanese woman who entered, chain-smoking evil-smelling cigarettes, and drove me into the streets.

I stood at the base of the old ramparts, atop the sloping stone embankment on the east bank of the river, where there is a good view to the north of its wide, curving sweep. The Rhône is one of France's mightiest rivers, almost nationalistic in its behavior. It begins its life as a Swiss river, born in the rugged Alps east of Geneva, and flows through peaceful Lac Leman. But after the fledging river crosses into France, it grows in strength and size. From the border it flows west and south to Lyon, where it turns south for good. In its course it carries the soil deposited by its many tributaries and pushes all this good French dirt from its vast marshy mouth out into the Mediterranean, expanding the territory of France into the sea. The town of Aigues-Mortes, originally built in 1240 by Louis IX, France's holiest king, as a seaport on the Mediterranean coast to launch Crusader ships toward Jerusalem, now lies five miles inland.

A strong breeze from the northwest rippled the water and, combined with the low and thick clouds, made for a nasty chill in the May air. The winding streets of the old quarter, milling with tourists, had been sheltered from the wind. On the exposed banks of the river with the wind in my ears, I stood alone. My plan and purpose were simple: to pursue the events of this thirteenth-century crusade ignited by Peter's death. To listen for their echoes. Do they still reverberate? Are there any remains of the brutal battles and massacres that followed Peter's murder? Or of the crusaders themselves and the heretics they pursued to the death across the medieval landscape of the Languedoc?

I should have been able to see the island in the middle of the Rhône that marks not only the point where the river splits into the Grand Rhône, on whose banks I stood, and the smaller Petit Rhône that meanders west to St-Gilles before it, too, joins the Mediterranean, but also where Peter of Castelnau was murdered on that January morning. The island wasn't there. I consulted my map and realized I had made an error. The point where the murder took place was at least five kilometers north.

I headed north in the Peugeot along the west bank of the river on the D15 toward Beaucaire, where Peter's murderer had fled. According to my Michelin map, the island lies opposite the little suburb of Fourques. I drove through the place, unable to find a road or path to the river. No monuments marked the spot of the murder. I passed a sign for a horseshoe maker. An obelisk on the north end of Fourques gave me hope. It was on the side of the road, an old stone pillar topped with a small and simple weathered iron cross. The monument honored a minister of France named Toulouse, a native son of Fourques, and dated from the 1840s. Only six hundred years off. On closer inspection I saw that the cross was made of two horseshoes that had been straightened and put at right angles to each other.

The D15 was a sweet road to drive, well paved and flat, with smooth curves that followed the riverbank, still hidden by rows of tall trees. On my left were small, well-kept fields in which the white horses of the Camargue grazed. I followed the D15 all the way to Beaucaire, turned around, and backtracked to Arles. I never found the spot where Peter was murdered.

The center of Arles belongs to the tourists. On the edge of the square that holds the city's famed Roman arena is the restaurant

L'Hôtellerie d'Arènes. Its bright, lace-curtained windows shone like smoky beacons through the darkness of evening. Madame, a sturdy woman with gray hair and a still-handsome face, dressed in a silky flowing skirt, swept the room with a wave of her arm. Only two tables were occupied. Sit anywhere. It was 7:00 P.M. and still early for dinner. (This remained my state—early for dinner and invariably one of the first patrons of whatever restaurant I chose. The closer I came to Spain, the later the dinner hour. In Toulouse I would wait, my stomach growling with complaint, until 9:30 and still be told, with a sweeping arm, "Sit anywhere.") I took a table at one of the shining windows. Madame approached, pencil and pad poised in her hands.

"Vous désirez?"

On her advice, I chose the evening's special, a regional stew called *daube,* made with bull meat and onions in a red wine sauce. With it came small white potatoes roasted with garlic. Madame also recommended a local beer. She wrote it all down in a spidery hand and retreated to the kitchen.

A French woman and her preteen daughter sat at a table next to me. The daughter was a miniature copy of the mother, both with straight reddish brown hair and thin, quick faces, like hungry foxes. The mother complained to the waitress, a plain, slim girl who sang not so quietly to herself as she fussed with the silverware at the empty tables. They had not ordered anything complicated. Her daughter was hungry. They had come in early because they had a train to catch. Why was their food taking so long? The waitress retreated and whispered in Madame's ear. Madame came forward. What was the problem? Didn't the customer know that each dish is individually prepared? The lady and her daughter drilled their eyes into Madame. "Quarante minutes est trop longue."

France is the land of food and a certain amount of time for

proper preparation is expected. That time had obviously been exceeded. Mother and daughter couldn't spend eternity waiting for two salads. More words were exchanged. Madame withdrew, her back straight and head high, the apparent winner, but the battle settled into a draw when the humming waitress appeared with their salads a scant minute thereafter.

My beer had been served promptly but I waited forty-five minutes for my stewed bull's meat. I didn't mind the time. It gave me the opportunity to look out my window at the first-century arena, a huge, hunched creature in the evening dim, and think about things.

The arena outside the restaurant window was built when Arles was a Roman town and France was still the Roman province of Gaul. In addition to arenas, amphitheaters, temples, aqueducts, and the rest, the Romans also built their famous system of roads that connected the settlements throughout Gaul to each other, to the rest of the Roman Empire, and eventually to Rome itself.

Anyone who has gone cross-country on a wet March day knows the value of a good road. No frozen clods of dirt to twist ankles, no pools of ankle-deep water to freeze feet and ruin shoes, no treacherously wet rocks to destroy footing. Roman roads were exceptionally good, usually three to four feet thick and built in layers of successively finer stone, each layer set in mortar, topped by a layer of sturdy, fitted stone. The proud Romans meant for them to last a millennium, and many did.

Arles was the strategic juncture of several of these Roman roads; the most important ran west to the vineyards of Narbonne and Toulouse and east to the Aurelian Way, which led to Rome. Originally built to facilitate trade and troop movement, the Roman roads through the south of Gaul carried much more than wine and soldiers. The roads through the Languedoc were still in use through most of the Middle Ages. For more than a millennium, streams of language, culture, and custom flowed over them in both directions. This east-west influence is still evident. From the west came the name for my evening's dinner. The word *daube* has Spanish origins. During the hot afternoons of the high summer months, Spanish-style bullfights—to the death—were held in the oval of the darkened arena outside my window. But even Roman roads could be dangerous, and one of the most dangerous travelers in these southern climes was the Cathar heresy, coming to the Languedoc in the tenth century from the east, through Bulgaria, Bosnia, and northern Italy.

Three of the greatest cities of thirteenth-century Europe were in the Languedoc. The three—Narbonne, Toulouse, and Montpellier—resembled the emerging city-states of Italy. Paris, the only city of any note in the north, was, except for its newly chartered university, a relatively unsophisticated backwater in comparison. The cities of the Languedoc were havens for uprooted people with different, even radical ideas—ideas such as those borne by the Cathars, whose beliefs stemmed from the concept of a universe divided into distinct and competing realms of good and evil.

In the thirteenth century, the Languedoc extended west from the Rhône to the Pyrenees and reached from the Mediterranean to the high, impassable plain of the Massif Central. Its name derives from the ancient language spoken there, *langue d'oc*. *Oc* was the southern word for yes. By contrast, in the northern region around Paris *langue d'oeil* was spoken. *Oeil*, also meaning yes, evolved into the modern French word *oui*. But language and the relative sophistication of their cities weren't the only differences between north and south.

The north of France had, over the previous centuries, developed the medieval feudal system and with it the system of primogeniture, whereby the firstborn male of the family inherited the wealth of his father in its entirety. Large estates in the north of France remained intact, ensuring strong centralized lord-vassal relationships. Second sons were forced to seek their fortune in the clergy or elsewhere. Social order remained in tight control of the higher nobles and a powerful clergy. Peter's order, the reformist Cistercians, founded in 1098 by Saint Robert of Molesme at Citeaux, had grown to be the most powerful in Europe, with more than three hundred monasteries throughout Europe by the beginning of the thirteenth century.

In comparison, the laws of inheritance in the Languedoc had remained as vestiges of old Roman law, which fit the southerners' more individualistic natures. All heirs, both men and women, shared equally in inherited wealth and property. As a result, medieval castles and fortifications were rarely the property of a sole noble. The castle at Mirepoix, for instance, was held in common by thirty-six knights, as was the castle of Montréal. An extreme case was the castle of Lombey, which was owned by fifty nobles. The walls surrounding the fortress city of Carcassonne were shared by sixteen noble families, each claiming its own tower. But the Languedoc was a land made rich by wine and the trade in woad, a medicinal herb whose leaves were the main source of the color blue for cloth dyers throughout Europe until the indigo plant arrived from India in the sixteenth century.

Many nobles could afford to build their own castle. There seems to have been one on almost every hilltop. Today, their ruins

serve as testaments to the Languedoc's stubborn history of indi-
viduality and desire for personal autonomy. They also serve, I
would discover, as a sore reminder of the south's inability to unite
itself for the sake of common defense.

The southern clergy did not shine when compared to the
churchmen in the north. The majority of the clergy of the Languedoc were either slackers or shysters. They much preferred
games of chance and hawking to hearing confessions, and rou-
tinely demanded payment from the faithful for dispensing the
sacraments to them, most particularly last rites. Southern clerics
were regularly lambasted for their greedy ways by the troubadours
that entertained at the complex network of small courts throughout the south. The thirteenth-century troubadour Peire Cardenal,
who sang at the grand court of Raymond VI, did not mince his
words:

> Buzzards and vultures
> do not smell out
> stinking flesh as fast
> as clerics and preachers
> smell out the rich.
>
> They circle round him, at once, like
> friends, and as soon as sickness
> strikes him down they get him to
> make a little donation, and his own
> family gets nothing.[1]

Any southern lord of importance in the thirteenth-century
Languedoc was bound to be named Raymond. The leaders of the
region's two most powerful families shared not only this surname
but a familial relationship as well. Raymond VI, the count of

Toulouse—the Raymond excommunicated by Peter of Castelnau—held lands extending in a lopsided rectangle from Toulouse to Nîmes and from Cahors to Narbonne, a town near the Mediterranean coast. Raymond-Roger Trencavel was the viscount of Béziers and Carcassonne and also the nephew of Raymond VI. The Trencavels held a rough triangle of territory anchored by the towns of Béziers, Carcassonne, and Albi. The Trencavel holdings thrust up into those of the count of Toulouse, effectively splitting the Toulousian lands in two. Although the counts of Toulouse were nominal overlords of the Trencavels, both families were rich and powerful, and their frequent, bloody struggles with each other constantly shifted the balance of power in the Languedoc back and forth between them.

Both of these Raymonds also named their eldest sons Raymond. It took some sorting out to get all the Raymonds in their proper relationships without too much slippage. In addition, a galaxy of lesser, but no less independent minded, nobles studded the Languedoc. There was the count of Foix, named Raymond-Roger (of course!), a fierce fighter whose domain was in the rugged foothills of the Pyrenees along the valley of the Ariège River. There were the count of Rodez, the viscounts of Narbonne and Montpellier, and various lords and sublords, all proud, all independent minded, and all self-serving, switching their allegiance from the house of Toulouse to the house of Trencavel and back again, at their convenience and for their momentary advantage.

All of the southern nobles of the Languedoc paid a nominal homage to the king of France, but the reality was that, in the thirteenth century, the north and the south of France functioned as separate countries, divided by unforgiving geography, differing customs and law, and a different language. Between the north and south lay the sparsely populated, isolated Massif Central, through which no roads or connecting rivers ran. The functional influence of the French king spread little beyond the area of the Île-de-France surrounding Paris or south of the Loire River valley.

My *daube* was excellent, with a delicate flavor, the potatoes hearty, the beer crisp and cold. I cleaned the last of the sauce from my plate with a final hunk of bread. Madame said she would not have to wash these dishes and asked if I desired some dessert. I chose an apple tart with coffee.

I paid the bill and thanked Madame for steering me toward the *daube*. She bowed me to the door, bade me good night, and I went out into the evening. More people were on the street now, many of them heading to the glowing facade of the small church of St. Julien of Arles. A poster advertised a choral concert this evening, benefiting the local league against cancer. Choruses from the towns of Stes-Maries-de-la-Mer, St-Martin, Arles, and Tarascon would be singing local folk songs, in both French and Provençal.

The *langue d'oc* suffered greatly at the close of the Albigensian Crusade, but it did not become extinct. Its descendant, modern Provençal, has enjoyed a renaissance in the south beginning early in the twentieth century, championed by the southern poet Frédéric Mistral. Mistral donated the proceeds from his 1904 Nobel Prize for Literature for a museum in Arles dedicated to Provençal life and language.

Two women, slim, eager, and birdlike, were collecting money and distributing tickets at a long table outside the church doors. They worked in smooth tandem with the ease of old confidantes, frequently leaning their heads together, the henna in their hair perfectly matched. I bought my ticket and one of them wished me "bonne chance"—good luck. The other saw the confusion on my face and pointed to a smaller sign I had not noticed. There was also to be a raffle that evening. First prize in the raffle was a week-long trip for two to Corsica. My ticket was entry to both. I went into the church.

The master of ceremonies was a slim man with elegant hair who wore a shiny tuxedo and held a large microphone. He was overactive, as are many hosts of variety shows on French television. He sang aloud with the choruses, implored the audience for greater applause, plunged into its midst, coaxing people to the front of the church and then abandoning them, leaving them to wander back to the seats from which they had been plucked.

The Provençal songs received the loudest ovations, uncoaxed by the man in the tuxedo. One song was titled "Lis Esclop" (The shoes), a traditional dance from the Languedoc. It elicited almost patriotic applause. I was reminded of the American South, where the strains of "Dixie" still bring an audience to its feet, and I unexpectedly grasped my first clear remnant of the thirteenth century, vibrating from the clear voices of the La Camarguenco chorus of Stes-Maries-de-la-Mer and echoing within the stone walls of the church.

After the singing came the raffle. A young couple with a small child won the trip to Corsica. The master of ceremonies bent down to the little girl, his voracious smile inches from her face, and offered to act as a baby-sitter for them. The parents looked horrified at the thought. The girl aimed a tiny kick at him, then retreated behind her mother's skirts. The audience howled with laughter. No, thank you. *Grandmère* would be delighted to care for *petite Cecile*.

Back in my hotel room I surfed through the television channels. An early-season bullfight in the Roman arena at Nîmes had made the evening news. The commentators spoke too swiftly and excitedly for me to understand, but the pictures were enough. A matador lay in the dirt of the ring, injured by the bull. A picador on horseback distracted and stabbed at the bull while the wounded matador was removed from the arena floor. The picador, a woman, returned to the lists to exchange horses. While remounting, she fell and was also injured. A second picador on a prancing horse now came out to confront the bull, a ton of brute confusion as he stood motionless, watching the picador through reddened eyes, flanks heaving with final breaths, bleeding, and dying in the center of the arena. The crowd was wild with applause and shouts. It was akin to the applause that I had heard in the church only a short time before, a salute to ancient tradition.

· T W O ·

The Abbey of St-Gilles

THE MOST DIRECT ROAD BETWEEN THE CITY OF ARLES AND
the town of St-Gilles, sixteen kilometers to the west, is the arrow-
straight, smooth N572, a *route nationale* that runs parallel to the
railway line between Arles and St-Gilles on the south bank of the
Petit Rhône. To the south of the N572 is the great green flatness of
the Tête de Camargue, the northern edge of the large triangular
marsh formed by the delta of the diverging Grand Rhône and
Petit Rhône. During the Middle Ages, monks from the Abbey of
St-Gilles panned salt from the marshes as a source of income. The
Camargue still produces salt, but the area is now more valued for
its tourist attractions, among which are the noble-looking white
horses of the Camargue. Several of them grazed in a distant field
behind a low fence. All was still in the Tête de Camargue except
for the tops of a few tall trees, leafy and full, tossing in the wind.

The last three kilometers on the north side of the N572, before
St-Gilles, prepared me for the town: mounds of gravel; the squat,
faceless buildings of an industrial zone, supply yards filled with
construction materials and large rolls of coiled cable standing
taller than the men who walked in front of them; a parking lot
holding battered yellow buses. The road into St-Gilles was gritty
and grim and made no attempt to welcome the visitor. Almost into
town the N572 crosses the Petite Rhône on an ungainly metal

bridge with wooden flooring and a weather-beaten sign advising drivers to "cross the bridge very slowly in case of rain, for it is very dangerous and slippery when wet." Then the road travels over a narrower stone bridge spanning the Rhône-Sète Canal, past a little harbor to the right of the bridge holding some rusty boats, and finally enters the hard-looking heart of the town of St-Gilles.

Tradition has it that Saint Gilles, the town's namesake, was a prosperous eighth-century Greek who decided one day to follow the life of a hermit. He distributed his money and all his possessions among the poor, climbed aboard a wooden raft, and floated away from his native land into the waters of the Mediterranean. The raft eventually bumped up against the shores of France and Gilles stepped off. In an unabashed foreshadowing of Francis of Assisi (who would not be born for another four hundred years), Gilles befriended many of the local animals, including one hind in particular. One day, Gilles saved the hind from the dinner table by snatching, in midflight with his bare hand, an arrow from a huntsman's bow. This feat so amazed the huntsman, a fellow of rich and noble birth, that on the spot he pledged both the land and the money for Gilles to establish an abbey on the site of the memorable event.

After the huntsman's generous pledge, Gilles journeyed to Rome to obtain recognition from the pope for his abbey. The pope presented him with two stout doors, made of wood and finely carved, for the abbey. Gilles proceeded to toss both doors into the Tiber River; they floated downstream and were carried into the Mediterranean, just as Gilles had been. The doors washed up not only at the very spot on the French shore to which Gilles had returned (by land this time) to fetch them up to the abbey, but at the very same time.

After a long life and still more miracles, Gilles died and was buried beneath the small church he had built. That church was eventually covered over by a much larger abbey, built in the twelfth century.

The abbey had been the site of confrontations between churchmen and heretics well before the beginning of the thirteenth century crusade against the Cathars. In the early 1130s, a Cathar heretic named Henry joined forces with an agitator and demagogue, Peter of Bruys, who was preaching his brand of theology to the towns of the southern Rhône valley. Peter, in common with Henry, disapproved of infant baptism and objected to both the celebration of feast days and the veneration of icons. Peter's career ended abruptly in front of the abbey when he attempted to set fire to a crucifix and was hung on the spot by the outraged monks of the abbey. Henry escaped and made his way to the relative safety of the region surrounding Toulouse, where he continued to preach the Cathar beliefs. Henry was eventually captured by the bishop of Toulouse and died in 1148 while still his prisoner.

The Abbey of St-Gilles continued to prosper until the Reformation, when parts of it were burned and several monks tossed down the abbey's well by zealous reformers. In 1622 the church belfry was destroyed by a fire. By the end of the eighteenth century, after more damage wrought by the antireligious excesses of the French Revolution, only the west facade of the medieval abbey remained intact.

⚜

The woman who showed me to my room at the Hôtel les Cabannettes, located just beyond the gravel piles on the N572, asked me if
I wanted to keep my car in the hotel's garage. Only forty francs
more per night. She pointed out that the corridor door to the outside was always locked for security. I tried the handles of the other
doors. Except for the front entry, the hotel was locked tight as a
drum.

Every French hotel seems to have a resident dog or cat. At the
Hôtel les Cabannettes, an aged German shepherd named Benni
lay either at the threshold of the front doors—requiring a ginger
stepping-around by staff and guests—or in the middle of the
lobby on the dark, cool tiles. Benni followed my passages through
the lobby with slow turns of his head.

The proprietress at the front desk asked again if I wanted a
garage space for the Peugeot. I told her that I didn't think it was
necessary. She pointed to the graveled lot at the front of the hotel
and shrugged at me. If I wasn't putting my car in the garage she
pointedly told me to take *everything* out of it.

After checking in, I went in search of the abbey. I parked next
to a blue Renault with a smashed-in rear window in the Place
Charles de Gaulle. It seemed like such a grand name for what
was only a large blacktop parking area posted with a few signs that
said parking was "gratuite et gardee 24H." I was in the middle of
St-Gilles but I couldn't find the abbey. No signposts, no church
spires, no bell towers guided me. I wandered by a sterile block
of concrete flats, five stories high, with men in front who smoked
and played endless games of *boules*. I wandered along a street
of sad restaurants with fly-specked windows. Houses were jum-
bled against each other, and apart from some shiny geraniums
civically planted in harsh concrete planters, the place was devoid
of flowers—no window boxes, no gardens. The only things I saw

on the main street were the shuttered shops of a Sunday afternoon and men slowly parading the streets in pairs or sitting almost motionless in cafés. I found the school, the brown soccer
field, but no abbey, or even signs for an abbey. How could a town
of only 11,000 people hide such a big old thing so well? Another
kind of town, one whose citizens planted flowers perhaps, would
have led me to it by the nose. Was it so forgotten that it was not
even worth a sign?

After more than an hour of walking, I finally asked a gray-
haired, red-faced man standing with a companion in front of the
Café de la Poste under a white bar/tabac sign. He didn't understand at first, then an interior light went on and shone in his eyes.
"Ah, l'Abbise." He pointed across the main street to two smaller
streets that diverged and climbed a hill, one to the left and the
other to the right. He waved his fist toward the one on the left.
"La," he said. That one. If I followed it I would find the abbey
"derrière l'église." Behind the church. I followed the street he had
pointed out and after several minutes of walking uphill saw a small
brown sign, stuck up on a brown crumbling wall of a building,
with an arrow to the "monuments de XIIs." I followed the arrow to
the tiny Place de la République. I never did see the church, but
there, its squat gray enormity dwarfing the square, was the Abbey
of St-Gilles.

On the stairs at the foot of the twelfth-century west facade sat
an even dozen bored tourists listening to a man who paced back
and forth before them, reading in loud monotone a description of
the abbey from the guidebook he held in his hands. The three
arched doorways, carved sometime between 1180 and 1240, all re-
late episodes in the life of Christ. The listeners looked at the man
and not the abbey. The man looked not at the abbey but at his
book. There was some logic to this. Most of the sculptural detail

of the building was eaten away. Stone faces worn to pitted nothingness, sculpted clothing crumbled to scraggly rags. It was in front of these doors that Raymond VI of Toulouse received his public scourging at the hands of the papal legate who succeeded Peter of Castelnau.

Despite the bitter meetings with Peter before Peter's murder, Raymond realized his need to quickly reconcile with the Church of Rome, especially in light of the military might of the crusader army that had gathered at Lyon during the spring and summer months of 1209. The crusaders had been whipped into a frenzy of religious zeal by Arnaud Amaury, the Cistercian chosen by Innocent III to be the papal representative and spiritual guide of the crusade.

Raymond sought reconciliation and the lifting of the excommunication pronounced by Peter two years before. In May of 1209, the count of Toulouse submitted himself to a public scourging by Milo, the monk named as Peter's successor as papal legate to the Languedoc. In addition to this combination of public humiliation and physical pain, Raymond was also required to forfeit a portion of his lands and a number of his castles to the church, and to swear an oath to take up the banner of the crusaders against the Cathars. This oath eventually proved to be only the first of many hollow words spoken during the crusade.

To the right of the facade were a pair of large metal doors, painted rusty red and swung wide, that opened on a path on the south side of the abbey to a door and down worn stone steps to the "lower church" and the crypt where the sarcophagus of Saint Gilles had been rediscovered during the middle of the nineteenth century.

Twenty feet above my head, the intricate ribs of the massive vaulted stone ceiling looked like they bore the whole weight of the world above and only God's intercession prevented it from falling down around one's ears. Down here, the thirteenth century did not feel that far away, even though these depths had been largely reconstructed after the Wars of Religion during the sixteenth century. A few small electric lights strung along the ceiling threw angled shadows into low corners.

Two women, caretakers, sat and tatted together without dropping a stitch in front of a wooden table that offered faded books about the abbey for sale. They hushed a noisy child running in a circle with a sharp command of "Silence!" They reminded me of my grade school nuns. Near the entry I peered through a metal grate down a forty-foot well that was near a wall containing a small niche. Within it, behind glass, a display of old bones, obviously human, had been arranged and backlit. Only two or three statues stood along the burdened walls. The crypt of Saint Gilles was in the center of the lower church, sunk five feet in the floor, surrounded by a three-foot-high iron fence wrought with curlicues.

An outstretched arm could reach over the fence, and the crypt was strewn with various items placed there by pilgrims. A dozen odd scraps of paper lay folded in two or wide open—prayers or requests for favors; two simple crosses, made of sticks crudely tied together; a pot of pink flowers; small sheaves of wheat tied into a tight bundle; a color photograph of a man and a woman, in their fifties perhaps, standing in a green mountain meadow with some cows in the background. Signs of a faith I had difficulty comprehending.

Heretics can hold a certain fascination for fallen-away Catholics, like me, who fall away not because they find a more appealing or compelling set of beliefs, but rather because they wind up believing in nothing in particular. In my case, it was not the devil that led me away but incredulity. I left the Catholic Church in my early teenage years, on the heels of my graduation from parochial grade school. As a result, my theology has never been very sophisticated, limited to the answers in my Baltimore Catechism and the oversimplified explanations provided by the good Franciscan nuns who taught me religion. They were much more successful at teaching me geography, spelling, and square roots.

The religion of my youth was a parade of miracles and mysteries. I could accept certain of them. A virgin giving birth. Water into wine at Cana. Lazarus rising. Loaves into fishes. The same sorts of happenings that, in one form or another, occupied the covers of supermarket tabloids. I certainly could have accepted the miraculous circumstances surrounding the founding of St-Gilles's abbey. After all, Superman was capable of catching bullets. A saint should be able to snatch an arrow in midflight.

But there were just too many mysteries to be gotten through. I stumbled badly at the notion of transubstantiation, the miraculous change by which bread and wine, when consecrated during a Catholic Mass, keep their outward appearance but actually become the Body and Blood of Christ. I could have accepted the idea of bread and wine as symbols of the Body and Blood, but the idea of consuming what was proclaimed to be human flesh and blood, even in different guise, was ghastly to me.

Transubstantiation was also a problem for the Cathars, but for different reasons. At the foundation of Cathar belief was the idea that the universe was divided into two distinct realms, one of good and one of evil. The spiritual realm was the realm of goodness and purity, created by God and containing him, the angels, and heaven. The realm of the material universe was created by the devil. Anything that could be touched, tasted, sniffed, eaten, seen, or heard was, by its physical nature, inherently evil. The logical trail that followed from this basic view of the universe could not help but lead to heresy in the eyes of the church. If the material world was the realm of evil, Christ as the Son of God could never really have descended to earth and become flesh and blood. The most he could have been was a spirit, only assuming a false corporeality. Never being born as flesh, never really human, he could not really have died for our sins. Nor have eaten a last supper. Nor have been resurrected on the third day. The whole idea of transubstantiation, the climax of the Catholic Mass, would become a meaningless deceit, along with many of the other orthodox beliefs of Rome.

A dualist view of the universe wasn't an invention of the thirteenth century. The religion founded by the Persian prophet Zoroaster in the seventh century B.C. had at its core not only the worship of a single god, Ahura Mazda, the "Lord Wisdom," but also a dualist struggle between Truth and Lie. Truth, including the creative force of the "Holy Spirit," emanates from Lord Wisdom. At the root of all evil is the "Fiendish Spirit," twin to the Holy Spirit. The Fiendish Spirit is evil because he has, by choice, allied himself with Lie. As the two spirits have chosen their sides, so must all humans choose. Upon death, all will be judged at the Bridge of Discrimination. Followers of Truth gain paradise. Followers of Lie are consigned to hell. All evil on earth will be consumed in a cataclysm of fire and molten metal.

Also from Persia came Manichaeism, established in the third century by the son of an aristocratic family of southern Babylonia. The son, Mani, inspired by revelations at the ages of twelve and twenty-four, proclaimed himself the last prophet in a line of succession that included Buddha, Zoroaster, and Jesus. Mani saw the universe divided into realms of good and evil. At the beginning of time, the spiritual realm of Light and the material realm of Darkness existed separately, but Darkness, ruled by Satan, invaded Light, ruled by God. The two realms collided. Humankind is not only the result of this perpetual struggle between Darkness and Light but also its reflection. The human body is evil; the human soul is part of the godly Light. In order for the soul to be released from its worldly imprisonment and gain the realm of Light, human desire, which perpetuates the soul's imprisonment, had to be defeated.

Manichaean missionaries journeyed east to China and west to the Roman Empire. The fourth-century theologian, Augustine, was a Manichaean prior to his conversion to Christianity, and the Manichaean influence in the West continued for centuries. In the seventh century were the dualist Paulicians who eventually merged with the Bogomils, another dualist sect that arose in the tenth century. The Bogomil doctrine differed in certain aspects from Manichaeism. The Bogomils held that the firstborn Son of God, called Satanel, rebelled against his father and created, in opposition to the original spiritual universe, the material world and the human beings who inhabit it. God the Father, however, invested these human beings with a "life spirit." This life spirit was kept enslaved by Satanel until the second Son of God, the Logos or Christ, descended from heaven, assumed a phantom body and broke the power of the evil Satan, whose signification of divinity, the *el* at the end of his name, was forever lost.

Early in the twelfth century, the Bogomil leader was executed and the heresy suppressed by the Catholic Church, but not before exerting its influence in France. Although the Paulicians, Bogomils, and other sects were all generally referred to as Cathars, the Greek for "pure," it was in southwestern France where the dualist doctrine reached a zenith. Here they were known as Albigenses, after the town of Albi, near Toulouse, where they were especially numerous and influential and where a Cathar bishop had been installed since the middle of the twelfth century. History has labeled the thirteenth century wars fought against them the Albigensian Crusade.

The Place de la République maintained the hard look of the town. The square where Raymond VI received his scourging and absolution at the hands of Milo was small and gray, perhaps fifty feet wide and seventy-five feet long. One skinny street led into it and one skinnier street led out. An attempt to replaster the facades of the buildings had failed to bring any charm to the place. There were still no flower boxes on the houses, only the perfunctory, oblong concrete planters out of which a few geraniums dared to show their heads.

Lining the square were a souvenir store, a dusty *salon de thé* that served pizza, the offices of an insurance company. Windows were streaked with dirt and walls faded against the blue sky. In one corner of the square broken concrete and triangular mounds of gravel—signs of continuing street repair—fronted a closed and grimy *boulangerie*. Fewer people were out and about up here on this Sunday afternoon than down the hill. The air was not hot, but the people moved with an August listlessness. Only the children in the square had any energy, but none of them smiled as they zoomed their bikes in and out of the square, shouting and chasing each other.

I went back down the hill to check on my Peugeot, which showed no signs of forced entry. It was now evening, and crowds of men packed the cafés. They were more animated, the buzzing chorus of their voices droning like mosquitoes at my ear, broken only by the occasional snap of a playing card. St-Gilles now seemed almost Middle Eastern; the women of the town kept themselves under wraps. I ate my invariably early meal at the hotel restaurant, Gillois, an unremarkable coq au vin with a chef's salad and a rosé from Aigues-Mortes.

By the twelfth century Catharism had become a dominant force in the Languedoc, largely owing to the laxity and corruption of the Roman Catholic clergy in the south of France. It was not that Rome had ignored the Cathars. As early as 1119, Pope Calixtus II condemned the heretics living in the area around Toulouse. In 1147, Pope Eugenius III sent the great Bernard of Clairvaux to the Languedoc to preach against the heresy, and in 1163, the Cathars were denounced at the Council of Tours. But these measures were ineffectual. It wasn't until one of the ablest and most powerful men of the Middle Ages assumed the papacy that the Cathars felt the hot breath of Rome on their necks.

Innocent III, born Lotario de' Conti di Segni in 1160, was the product of two noble Italian families. He received the finest education the Middle Ages offered, studying theology in Paris and canon law in Bologna. Because of his noble lineage, he had powerful connections in Rome. Even though he had never been ordained as a priest, he was unanimously chosen to succeed the undistinguished Pope Celestine III, who had died in 1198. After a hasty ordination on 21 February 1199, Lotario was elevated to the papacy the next day, choosing the name Innocent III. The new pope proved intelligent, resolute, indomitably willful, skilled in the handling of men, arrogant, and eminently practical. He was a man born to wield power and saw himself "set midway between God and man. Below God but above man."[2]

The few paintings of him that exist, executed a century after his death, bear out a contemporary description of Innocent III having a "pale oval face, long dominating nose, oblique eyes, tiny ascetic mouth forceful chin."[3] The lack of modern perspective in medieval art and the convention of making the most important person in the picture the largest combine to conceal Innocent's relative lack of physical stature. He was Napoleonically short.

Innocent's first step in combating the Cathars was to appoint members of the Cistercian order knowledgeable in Catholic doctrine to replace the lazy and untrained clerics in the Languedoc. The French Cistercians were eventually joined by two Spanish preachers, Bishop Diego of Osma and Domingo de Guzmán, the future Saint Dominic.

Innocent III had made the crusading pot too sweet to resist. Any man taking up the cross against the Cathars in the Languedoc for a period of forty days or more was to receive full crusading privileges, just as if he had undertaken the long and perilous trip to the Holy Land to wrest Jerusalem from the Moslems. Remission of all past sins. The right to claim any booty captured in battle. And most important, for the land-hungry nobles of the north, the right to any lands confiscated from those who sheltered the heretics. In the eyes of Arnaud Amaury and his crusaders, the lands of the Trencavel family were as legitimate a target as those of

Raymond VI, as Raymond-Roger made no secret of his sympathy
for the Cathars who found refuge in his domain.

By the end of June 1209, the crusaders were ready to march
south. Riding at the head of the army beside the papal legate
Arnaud Amaury were the duke of Burgundy and the counts of
St-Pol and Nevers, the most powerful lords of northern France
save for the king. In the early days of July 1209, the marching
banners were unfurled. Singing "Veni Sancti Spiritus," a rous-
ing hymn composed by Innocent III that was to become the an-
them of the crusade, the army marched out of Lyon and made its
way in holy resolution down the Rhône River valley to the
Languedoc. Now that Raymond VI was reconciled with the
church and safely returned to the fold, the full force of the crusaders was deflected away from the lands of the count of Toulouse
and toward those of Raymond's chief rival in the Languedoc, his
youthful nephew, Raymond-Roger Trencavel, the viscount of
Béziers and Carcassonne.

The morning after I visited the abbey, Benni wandered into the
breakfast room. Usually French dogs are polite and mind their own
business. But Benni came up to my table and began gently butting
my leg with his head. The usually harried barman hastened to my
table. Please excuse Benni. The barman held up a hand and covered his eyes, then placed it over Benni's. "Il ne vois pas." Benni
was blind. The barman led Benni away like a tender pied piper—
using the soft sound of his voice, calling Benni's name gently—to
his usual spot on the cool lobby tiles. When I left the breakfast
room and stepped around Benni, he didn't follow my sounds with
his head. There was no need, the barman said. He knew me now.

I had felt trapped by St-Gilles. It was a joyless, unpleasant town and it stretched out its grim fingers to encompass me. I wanted something nice to remember and now I could remember Benni and the barman and their mutual patience, kindness, and trust. With the discovery of this redeeming value, a good memory of St-Gilles, I was free to leave it.

THREE

The Destruction of Béziers

IN THE COURSE OF THE CRUSADERS' MARCH SOUTH, A DOZEN castles along the Rhône valley surrendered to them without resistance. At the town of Valence, Raymond VI joined their number, leading them across the newly built Pont-St-Bénézet at Avignon to the western shore of the river. By mid-July, the crusaders had reached the city of Montpellier, since 1205 a part of the kingdom of Aragon through marriage. The leaders of the crusade were met by an overwhelmed and, to all appearances, contrite Raymond-Roger Trencavel.

Raymond-Roger had come into both his title and full inheritance at the age of nine. His youthfulness meant that he was able to exert little or no control over his vassals. Bernard de Saissac, the regent who ruled for Raymond-Roger before he gained his majority, was a Cathar, and many of his other subjects not only became followers of the Cathar way but also turned their individual castles and hilltop towns into sorts of semiautonomous minikingdoms. Raymond-Roger maintained true control only over the cities of Béziers and Carcassonne. Although he had grown into a charming and assured young nobleman, the epitome of a medieval gallant, he held little sway in his domain. When Raymond-Roger met Arnaud Amaury at Montpellier, he was but twenty-four years of age and had been caught totally off-guard by his uncle's reconciliation with the Catholic Church and the humiliation he allowed himself to endure at St-Gilles.

Now, awed by the strength of the crusaders' army, Raymond-Roger finally understood his uncle's actions and comprehended his own desperate straits. He explained to Arnaud Amaury that he himself was certainly no heretic and pleaded that, because of his inexperience and early ascension to power, he could not be held accountable for his lack of control over his subjects. Raymond-Roger expressed his willingness to submit himself to the church, as his uncle had done. Arnaud Amaury, his army primed for battle, would hear none of it. The crusaders would march on Béziers presently, and he summarily dismissed Raymond-Roger from his presence.

The young viscount, knowing Montpellier was only a two-day march from Béziers, his largest city, rode through the night on horseback. He hastily called the citizens of Béziers together and, after directing them to defend the city to the best of their ability, rode to muster his forces at Carcassonne, one of the best-defended cities in the Languedoc and Raymond-Roger's stronghold.

The N572 continues west from St-Gilles for thirty kilometers and runs parallel to the railway line through flat land crisscrossed by canals until it connects in a slanted T with the Autoroute Languedocienne that runs south and west from the Rhône valley at Orange to Perpignan, the Mediterranean doorstep of the Pyrenees. From the cross of the T, it is twenty-four kilometers to Montpellier, today a university town and capital of the lower Languedoc. West of Montpellier, the names of the towns sound less French: Aigean,

Poussan, Bouzig, Pézenas. From Montpellier to Béziers is sixty kilometers. This is the route to Béziers that the crusaders in all probability followed, the easiest and the most direct, skirting the north end of the marshes and lagoons that string out along the Mediterranean coastline. What in the thirteenth century took two days of hard march takes slightly less than one-half hour on the Autoroute Languedocienne, if the traffic is slow.

But I didn't follow the autoroute. I went south instead, along the western edge of the Camargue, heading toward the Mediterranean by way of Aigues-Mortes, the thirteenth-century town that Louis IX built. It is a showpiece of late-thirteenth-century town planning, one of the earliest bastides. Its outer walls make a perfect square, and its grid of straight streets, meeting at right angles, facilitates the flow of commerce or troops.

West of Aigues-Mortes, the coast road is lined with modern resorts built during the 1960s and 1970s. The biggest are La Grande-Motte, with its pyramid housing, and Cap d'Agde. Thirty years ago the site of Cap d'Agde, at the end of a curving peninsula, was a desolate, marshy salt plain. Today there are flats and apartments and resort hotels painted either pink or blue, harbors for pleasure boats, and a quay lined with cheap, repetitive restaurants that serve tourists pizza, crêpes, ice cream creations, and *fruits de mer*. But Cap d'Agde is old, too. The Greeks were here before the Romans, and one of their statues, a male nude that was discovered in the nineteenth century still in its crate on a sunken ship, is the centerpiece of the Musée de l'Ephèbe in Cap d'Agde. Ten kilometers inland from the modern Cap d'Agde is the old town of Agde, on the Hérault River.

⚜

Innocent III appointed one of his hard-nosed Cistercians, Theodisius, as bishop of Agde early in the thirteenth century after removing his lax predecessor. The Hérault marked the eastern
border of the lands of Raymond-Roger Trencavel. If I were a crusader, I would now be in enemy territory, armed with the pope's
declaration of open season on Cathars and their Catholic sympathizers. Any booty I took in battle would be rightfully mine with
the blessings of Mother Church.

On 21 July 1209, the crusaders crossed the Hérault. The town of
Servian, thirteen kilometers northwest of Béziers, surrendered
without resistance. Arnaud Amaury directed the bishop of Béziers,
who had accompanied Raymond-Roger to Montpellier, to return
to his city and present its citizens with an ultimatum. The townspeople crowded into the Cathedral of St-Nazaire, located on the
strong, rocky escarpment high above the river Orb and dominating
both the river and the old Roman bridge that crossed it.

The bishop spoke to them of the great strength and fierce de-
termination of the crusaders and pleaded with them to surrender
without a struggle. He presented them a list with the names of two
hundred heretics known to be living in Béziers. If the two hundred
were given up to the crusaders, the Catholics of the town would be
spared and their property respected. Otherwise, the bishop
warned, they would find themselves confronting an overwhelming
military force that would grant them no quarter.

The first thing I found in Béziers was a traffic jam on rue Président
Wilson. I nosed my Peugeot to the Place Jean-Jaurès, a pleasant
grassy park accented with wrought-iron benches, geometric rows
of poplars and well-tended flower beds, and three levels of parking

underneath. I judged from the traffic, the bustle of the streets, and the number of fancy sedans parked underground that Béziers prospered and that its 76,000 residents, the Bitterois as they call themselves, were fat and happy.

From the Place Jean-Jaurès the streets rose up steadily in lazy curves and were lined with three- and four-story houses of either stone or brick. I made my way up the sloping streets. Steady streams of traffic filled them and a number of small dogs stood at the tall open windows of the houses, forepaws on sills, watching my progress. There were no signs of the old city walls or the town's medieval gates. However, the *langue d'oc* was evident. The street signs were in both French and Occitan (as the *langue d'oc* is called here). A brochure obtained at the tourist bureau claimed that 48 percent of the local population understand Occitan and that close to 30 percent can speak it. Schools have been founded to teach the Occitan language to children in nearly all the villages in the vicinity of Béziers, and an Occitan presence on the Internet is being established.

A sudden, sharp turn, past a poodle calmly surveying life from the fourth floor, put me at one end of a small plaza. At the other end was the Cathedral of St-Nazaire. In the plaza, women promenaded with their dogs and civil servants tended flower beds and watered shrubs in round concrete tubs. The Brasserie du Palais, its semicircular terrace shaded by fat leafy trees, was two-thirds filled. A hexagonal stone fountain burbled a spring of water from a rusted spigot. Over the square loomed one massive flank of the rear wall of the cathedral, the base stones comprising its oldest section.

The front of the cathedral, opposite the walls nearest the Brasserie du Palais, faces onto a terrace of its own, called the Plan dels Albigeses in Occitan. A promenade followed the top of the escarpment above the treetops and provided good views of the Orb below, the old bridgehead that carried the Roman road over it, and the red-tiled roofs of the low houses across the river. Spillways now regulate the flow of the river upstream of the Pont-Vieux. Beyond was the great flat valley of the Orb and in the distance the rising hills of the Haut Languedoc to the west and north.

With the exception of the intricate rose window that graced its upper reaches, the facade of the cathedral that faced the river was more fortress than church, with narrow slits of windows more appropriate for shooting arrows out than letting light in. An old man, bent and walking with a cane but still dapper in a hat and striped blue suit, approached me and began all at once to give me a lesson. He waved the tip of his cane at the curved wall closest to the Brasserie du Palais. "C'est d'origine," he said. Original. He made a sweep over the rest of the cathedral. "C'est du quatorzième siècle." The rest was from the fourteenth century. I asked him if he was from Béziers, but he only repeated his short lesson, word for word. He turned and began walking away. I called out a thank-you at his retreating figure. He lifted his cane and waved the tip in small circles, then continued down the hill, past the brasserie, and out of sight.

After listening to the grave ultimatum of their bishop, the citizens of Béziers consulted among themselves. Their town was built on a cliff fortified by stout walls and was well stocked with food and water. They reasoned that the town could easily withstand a siege of forty days. By that time, the crusaders would have exhausted the local supplies of food available to them and be forced to raise the siege. Many of them would leave because their forty-day commit-

ment would be at its end. In any event, the town expected reinforcements led by Raymond-Roger to arrive from Carcassonne in
short order. The citizens refused the terms of surrender laid out by
their bishop.

We will never know if their reasoning was sound. The bishop
departed the city accompanied by the handful of citizens who had
no stomach to defy the crusaders. He would have to report to Arnaud Amaury the city's refusal to surrender its Cathars. But as soon
as the bishop passed beyond the town gate, a small group of the
citizen-defenders, already whipped into fighting spirit, sortied beyond the city walls before adequate defenses were in place and fired
a shower of arrows at the crusaders and their mercenaries who were
establishing an encampment at the foot of the walls. An arrow
felled one of their number. The mercenaries, incensed by this
"sneak attack," stormed the gate on the heels of the sortie's hasty
retreat. The bells of the city sounded the alarm, but the citizens,
panicked at the ferocity and the swiftness of the counterattack,
abandoned their battle posts and fled to the cathedral and the other
churches, seeking sanctuary. The gate was quickly breached and
the mercenaries poured into the city, followed by the crusaders.

It was then that the horror of Béziers began. Once within the
walls, the mercenaries began an indiscriminate slaughter. They
killed in the houses and on the streets. They killed men and
women, children, priests, heretics, and true believers. Those who
had sought refuge in the houses of God met the same fate. In the
course of the killing, the mercenaries lit firebrands and began to
burn the city. Fire caught the roof of the cathedral. It collapsed in
a flaming heap upon those who lay dead or dying on the blood-
slick cathedral floor.

According to the songs of Guirat Riquer, a troubadour born
twenty years after the massacre, more than seven thousand people

were hacked, run through, bludgeoned, or burned to death by the forces from the north. Only when the mercenaries tried to claim the loot of the dead for themselves did the crusaders intervene and stop them. In all, the killing took less than three hours. A small plaque on the stone wall opposite the entry to the church commemorates the events of that July day, calling it the "Grand Mazel." The great butchering.

Above the entry was a carving of the brutal beheading of Nazaire, the patron saint of the cathedral, at the hands of the Romans. I donated two francs for a visitor's guide and headed for the cathedral's oldest corner, the Chapel of the Virgin, whose stone walls date from before the thirteenth century and witnessed the massacre. I couldn't resist running my hands over their rough surfaces. It was an instant and immediate connection to the crusaders and the Cathars, my first physical connection with the medieval brutality that I would revisit again and again in the coming days. The cathedral was beautiful and seemed at peace in twentieth-century Béziers, but now my mind imagined it eight hundred years ago, filled with wailing, bleeding people, the burning vaults of the roof crashing down upon the dying and the dead.

On the other side of the cathedral on a simple stone slab rests a sculpture of the body of Christ. The sculpture, broken through at the knees and the torso, also witnessed the massacre. Atop one of the original columns, just at the point where the wall met the vaulted ceiling on its climb toward heaven, a gargoyle was carved into the capital. It was a winged creature with two heads, one of a man and the other of a sly devil with pointed ears. Both man and devil had lips pulled back and teeth bared. It was only after I gazed at it for several minutes that I realized the man was crying out in despair but the devil was smiling.

The interior of the cathedral has been layered over, decorated and redecorated throughout the years, with faded Italian frescoes from the fourteenth century (a reflection of the papacy's relocation to Avignon that century), a sacristy ceiling from the fifteenth, altar from the sixteenth, choir and organ from the seventeenth. A tour group clomped through the doors and across the stone floor, thirty-plus people, noisy and distracting by sheer force of number. They arranged themselves at the front of the church on the wooden chairs. A Frenchman, a professor at a local university, stood in front of them and pointed at a portion of wall or a stained glass window. Necks craned in semicircles and video cameras panned. The Frenchman recited dates and architectural styles to the group, translated into English by the tour leader, who stood at the Frenchman's side. There was no mention of the Cathars or that day in July 1209. The group was quiet and respectful but also impatient. They rose in a mass rustle and hurried through the gate in the communion rail, video cameras at the ready to admire the complicated late Gothic ceiling of the sacristy before returning to their bus.

I could have followed along, but something from Catholic grade school made the other side of the communion rail off limits for me. Before I went out into the afternoon sunshine, I dropped a five-franc coin into a rattly metal box, lit a candle, and placed it in front of the Chapel of the Virgin, near the walls I had touched.

What could possibly be said in the aftermath of such complete destruction, so much death in so short a time? In his report to Innocent III, Arnaud Amaury summed up the events at Béziers succinctly and dispassionately. "Neither age nor sex nor status has been spared," he wrote.

Historians have debated for years whether or not the massacre at Béziers was a spontaneous display of blood lust or a plan of battle decided upon prior to the slaughter, an object lesson for other towns that might choose to resist. Before the attack, Arnaud Amaury reputedly declared, "Kill them all! God will know his own." We do not know if this carnage was a deliberate plan. We do know, however, that with the smell of blood and the smoldering city and the burned flesh fresh in their nostrils, the crusaders resolved that, wherever they met with resistance, the entire population would suffer the same fate as the people of Béziers.

Sitting in the shade of the Brasserie du Palais, I asked the waitress about the bilingual street signs. She tugged at her pulled-back hair. Her information differed from the tourist brochure. She told me that only the "trés agé," the very old, spoke Occitan now, and that only one school continued to teach it to "les petits," the little ones.

"It will soon be a lost language," she said. I pointed out that people had been saying that about Occitan for eight hundred years. I asked her if she spoke it.

"Mais, non. Je suis du nord."

FOUR

The Siege of Carcassonne

THE CRUSADERS REMAINED AT BÉZIERS FOR THREE DAYS
after the slaughter. During that time representatives from the
town of Narbonne presented themselves to Arnaud Amaury and
offered to surrender the Cathars in their midst. After decamping,
the army was in high spirits as they marched west along the Aude
River in pursuit of Raymond-Roger Trencavel. They encountered
no resistance on their route, only deserted towns and villages
whose inhabitants had fled either to the hills or to the protecting
walls of Carcassonne. Some towns were stoutly fortified and had
they offered any resistance, they could have slowed the crusaders'
march to Carcassonne, giving Raymond-Roger more time to prepare his city's defenses.

But as it was, an advance party of crusaders covered the ninety-
kilometer distance from Béziers in six days, a rapid pace for a pon-
derous thirteenth-century army on the march, especially in the
exceptional heat of the summer of 1209. They arrived at the walls
of Carcassonne on 28 July. By 1 August, the main body of the army
was encamped around the city and the siege began.

The land between Béziers and Carcassonne is comely. Vineyards line the main roads and extend to the distant, rising slopes. The land is green and bountiful. No wonder the crusaders coveted it.

From the beginning, Carcassonne divided me. It seemed the best of places from a distance, where the entirety of the old walled town, known as the Cité, can be viewed, plunked down perfectly on its hilltop, straight-flanked stone walls and circular towers rising above the tossing trees of the slopes below.

A good place for this medieval view of Carcassonne is from an exclusive twentieth-century vantage point, a rest stop on the Autoroute des Deux Mers that connects the cities of Marseilles and Toulouse. The ground is high, with a small stand of trees for cool shade and a wide view across the Aude valley. When I first saw the Cité from this spot it appeared frozen in time, its isolation enhancing a medieval purity, an eternal image in shimmering stone set against the patchwork green of the hillside and the burning blue of the southern sky. The world shrank to the hot southern sun on my neck and the tops of the trees roused by the wind and the fabulous walled city. A medieval pilgrim making his footsore way to a holy shrine might have seen it exactly as I was seeing it then.

But my Michelin Guide told me that a thoroughly modern city spread out beyond the walls and towers of the hilltop Cité and across the Aude, that it was home to 43,000 people, with an economy built on the rather mundane pursuits of leather tanning and the manufacture of hosiery. The guide also told me the Cité was the third most popular tourist attraction in France, behind only Paris and Mont-St-Michel in Brittany. So I knew that busloads of day-trippers stormed the place on a daily basis during high season, in numbers sufficient to support a trove of tacky T-shirt and cheap souvenir shops.

What I saw from the rest stop on the autoroute was an illusion.

The height of the dancing trees and the distant point from which I observed and the brilliant blueness of the sky all conspired to hide the modern city that lay at the foot of the white walls, to make the busloads of tourists disappear, to carry me back in time. But this knowledge did not change the timelessness I felt while viewing Carcassonne. Instead, the twentieth century lost some of its firm grip on me. I saw myself, in this brief but eternal moment, as a sort of time traveler, able to move back and forth between the firm present and the distant, veiled past.

Once within the walls, the Cité is best experienced on the edges of the night, when the fumy buses have departed with their burdens and the souvenir shops and antique stores, the street food counters and T-shirt stands hide behind barred doors and shuttered windows. Dawn is better than evening, when there is less chance of encountering a band of exuberant teenagers or drunk and stumbling tourists, their blurry, boisterous voices magnified by the narrow streets and empty squares and ricocheting off the stone walls and into the quiet night air. It is then that the outer ramparts encircling the Cité reclaim their medieval dignity and power and their circumnavigation, a two-and-one-half-kilometer walk along the parapets and watchtowers, brings forth a quiet contemplation of the land below and beyond and the walled city within and the unforgiving march of time.

There have been walls on the hilltop of Carcassonne since Roman times, when a wooden fort guarded the road the wine merchants traveled between Narbonne and Toulouse. In the fifth century, the era that dates the earliest stone foundations, Carcassonne belonged, alternately, to the Romans or the Visigoths. Early in the eighth century, the city was in the hands of Saracens from Spain but was recaptured for Christianity by Charlemagne.

The fortifications were expanded and improved late in the thirteenth century in the aftermath of the Albigensian Crusade. For four hundred years the Cité was a bulwark against further invasions from Spain. But after 1659, when a treaty between France and Spain firmly established the border between the two countries well to the south of Carcassonne, the military importance of the Cité diminished. Walls and towers fell into woeful disrepair. The hilltop was all but abandoned and regularly raided to supply building materials for the prosperous and expanding Lower Town.

Credit for the restoration of the Cité belongs to the French architect Eugène-Emmanuel Viollet-le-Duc. Born in 1814 into a wealthy and progressive family, he exhibited an independent streak early on, refusing to attend the de rigueur École des Beaux-Arts and opting instead to study architecture in Italy. Inspired by Victor Hugo and his *Notre-Dame de Paris,* Viollet-le-Duc established himself as an authority on the architecture of the French Middle Ages. His destiny was sealed by a meeting with the French author and freshly appointed inspector for the newly founded Commission des Monuments Historiques, Prosper Mérimée. With the encouragement and support of Mérimée, Viollet-le-Duc received his first commission in 1840, the restoration of the crumbling eleventh-century Basilica of Ste-Madeleine at Vézelay. Restorations of the Ste-Chappelle and Notre-Dame in Paris soon followed. For the next forty years, Viollet-le-Duc was everywhere. At times it seems there is not an old rampart, tower, castle, battlement, or crenellated wall in all of France, and especially in the Languedoc, that has not been rebuilt or reshaped by his hand. In 1844, he was commissioned to restore the Basilica of St-Nazaire in Carcassonne. Again with the support of Mérimée, he convinced the commission that the entirety of the medieval Cité deserved restoration. This work began in 1855. Viollet-le-Duc died in 1879, with the restoration still in progress. It was completed by his students in 1898.

As restored by Viollet-le-Duc, a double wall of ramparts studded with thirty-five defensive towers encircles the Cité. Two gates give entry, the Porte Narbonnaise to the east and the Porte d'Aude leading to the river on the west. The inner ramparts are built higher than the outer, a clever design that allowed for defense of the city from both simultaneously. Between the ramparts are the *lices*, or lists, wide swaths of green spaces. Used for tournaments and games in times of peace, the *lices* afforded no protection for an enemy who had breached the outer wall. In a typical bureaucratic tangle, the state of France owns and maintains the town walls and the *lices* and also the Château Comtal within the walls. The city of Carcassonne is responsible for maintaining the rest of the Cité.

How faithful was Viollet-le-Duc's restoration of the Cité? Some critics claim that it is not an authentic reflection of the architecture of southern France in medieval times. This criticism is perhaps more indicative of old north/south prejudices than a comment on architectural style. Viollet-le-Duc was born and raised in the north of France. Therefore, the critics argue, he could not possess the proper empathy for the Languedoc to make his work at Carcassonne either truly authentic or acceptable. In fact, Viollet-le-Duc used local artisans—masons, stonecutters, blacksmiths, sculptors, and carpenters—whenever he could in the restoration of the Cité. Argument regarding his work continued back and forth, but the restoration of the Cité swayed one critic. Henry James, the nineteenth-century American author and traveler, was usually no friend to the work of restorationists, much preferring the "reality of undisturbed ruins." Yet he admitted that Viollet-le-Duc's work was "a splendid achievement."

Today, the Cité makes its living selling the Middle Ages. Among its wares are acres of T-shirts, mountains of souvenir coffee cups, truckloads of tiny spoons, all adorned with the fleury, a kind of cross, the end points stylized with fleurs-de-lys, that has become the Cathar symbol. Plastic swords and helmets, also adorned with Cathar crosses, are heaped in shop windows. Boys hold mock battles everywhere. No matter that scholars believe the Cathars were pacifists.

The take-away special at the fast-food counter near the Porte Narbonnaise was a "panini Cathar" and Coca-Cola for fifteen francs. The panini, a sandwich of goat cheese and tomatoes, was at least true to the modern idea that the thirteenth-century Cathars were practicing vegetarians. The sandwiches looked delicious, though any enjoyment they brought in that regard would have been in conflict with the Cathars' rejection of all sensual pleasure as evil.

The worst of Carcassonne panders to the prurient, and the worst by far is the Musée de l'Inquistion et Instruments de Torture on the rue de Grand Puits. Its air is less museum and more carnival sideshow. A tall blond in blue jeans hawked the place, coming out into the middle of the street to snag me. "You speak French? English? German?" She plucked at my sleeve. "Come in. Lots to see. You won't be sorry." It sounded like the recitation of a pimp.

The cover of the brochure she shoved into my hand featured a picture of a heavy, wooden chair with a high, straight back, equipped with a foot plate and manacles for hands and feet. Its back, sides, arms, seat, legs, and foot plate—anywhere the body would touch—was a bristly mass of sharpened metal spikes. The devices touted on the inner pages were equally ghastly: a hideous iron mask; a metal spike sharpened at both ends, secured to a metal ring that encircled the neck and designed to be lodged between the chin and breastbone—any movement, any dropping of the chin in exhaustion or just plain misery would rend the flesh; combination leg and arm irons designed to collapse and hold the wearer in a cramped fetal position.

Neither the hawker nor her brochure enticed me to enter.

In amusing juxtaposition to the torture museum was the Musée International de Dessin Animé—the cartoon museum. It featured the works of both Tex Avery and Walt Disney, who is said to have drawn inspiration from the Cité for the sets of his *Sleeping Beauty*.

The massive Château Comtal takes up a large portion of the space within the walls of the Cité. Built by the Trencavel family in the eleventh century, it is a fortress-within-a-fortress with its own system of gates and moats. Viollet-le-Duc paid special attention to the reconstruction of the château's "hoardings," special trapdoors for dropping stones and missiles on any invader who had managed to fight his way past both the inner and the outer ramparts. My tour guide was a diminutive trainee whose English was a burden to American ears. "Dysentery" sounded like "this century." She also upped the number of dead at Béziers to 20,000, an example of tourist-driven inflation.

Raymond-Roger had been busy the ten days since he departed Béziers. It seems paradoxical that his medieval preparations for defense entailed so much destruction. Portions of St-Nazaire were dismantled, the stone used to plug gaps in the Cité's fortifications. All foodstuffs in the surrounding area that couldn't be carted into the city were set to the torch. The floating water mills in the Aude River, vital to the normal life of the city, were smashed to bits to prevent the crusaders from milling the grain they carried with them.

Initially, the crusaders faced a daunting task. Carcassonne was strong and would be stubbornly defended. After careful consideration, they chose to attack at the one point of weakness they perceived. The first battle was for the unfortified suburb of St-Vincent that lay to the west of the Cité between it and the river. St-Vincent was captured with relative ease, and the Cité was effectively cut off from its surface water supply. Raymond-Roger had to rely upon the cisterns and the deep wells sunk within the Cité's walls. After the relatively easy capture of St-Vincent, the crusaders turned their attention to the fortified suburbs at the foot of the main walls, the bourg on the north and the castellare on the south. Here, resistance stiffened and the fighting became difficult. The bourg fell to the crusaders on 3 August. The next day, they launched a fierce but unsuccessful attack on the castellare, and were beaten back by flights of arrows and stones rained down upon them from the top of the walls. During the failed assault one of the crusaders in particular, a minor baron from the Île-de-France named Simon de Montfort, showed noteworthy courage by leading the first wave of knights in the initial attack and pulling a wounded comrade to safety during the retreat that followed. On 7 August, the castellare was taken by the crusaders in a heated struggle, but it was won back by Raymond-Roger in bitter fighting the next day.

The siege continued in a bloody, seesaw stalemate for seven

more days. In the end it was not any military stratagem but the extreme heat of August 1209 that conspired to bring the crusaders victory. That August was the hottest and driest in living memory. Carcassonne, overcrowded with refugees from the valley, depleted the already low wells. No rain fell to replenish the cisterns. Throats cracked and bled as both men and animals began to die of thirst. Disease spread. The stench coming over the walls from the city became intolerable, one crusader observed. Further resistance would soon be impossible, and Carcassonne would fall without mercy.

Then, in the darkest hours, from the heights of the walls the defenders of the Cité saw a miracle of sorts riding toward them over the plain. It was Peter II, the king of Aragon, at the head of a large contingent of his Spanish knights. Peter ruled the city of Montpellier in the Languedoc, recently acquired through marriage. The king was no great friend of the southern nobility and was himself a proud Catholic—he was about to undertake a crusade in Spain against the Saracens—but he looked upon the northern crusaders as invaders in a territory where he held a proprietary interest.

Peter interceded with the crusaders on Raymond-Roger's behalf and secured a promise of safe passage for the young viscount to negotiate terms of surrender. In light of the events at Béziers, the demands of Arnaud Amaury were surprisingly mild, perhaps owing to the intercession of the Aragonese king. All the inhabitants of the Cité, both Catholic and Cathar, were required to depart immediately. All of their property was forfeit, taken as booty by the crusaders. The Cité would come under control of the crusaders.

Despite the promise of a safe passage, Raymond-Roger was seized at the end of the day-long negotiations, shackled, and led to a nearby prison, where he died that November of the dysentery the tour guide at the Château Comtal had difficulty pronouncing.

Notwithstanding this final deceiving of Raymond-Roger, the crusaders held to their other promises and the inhabitants of the Cité left the walled town peacefully the next day, wearing, as a contemporary chronicler noted, "only their sins."[4] The victors entered. The looting that followed was systematic, and the Cité was spared the torch. Carcassonne had escaped the fate of Béziers. Within the walls of St-Nazaire, the crusaders gave praise and thanked God for their victory.

I found remnants of both Cathar and crusader within St-Nazaire. St-Nazaire is now officially a basilica, since it lost its status as a cathedral to St-Michel in the Lower Town in 1803. A plaque on the wall told me the great Saint Dominic preached there in 1213 while the Albigensian Crusade still raged across the Languedoc. The basilica is in the shape of a cross, with only portions of the ceiling vaults and walls of the long nave remaining from the structure that stood in the thirteenth century. Along with new stone, paint and sculpture have been added over the centuries, as in the cathedral at Béziers and most other Romanesque churches in France. And there was also Viollet-le-Duc's restoration to consider. But I paid a franc for a brochure and it led me directly to the thirteenth-century Notre-Dame Chapel on the northern flank of the altar and its rich stained glass window. Stained glass windows acted as medieval books, meant not only to glorify but instruct. The figures rising from bottom to top represent the family tree of Jesse, the father of King David of Israel, thereby depicting the human genealogy of Jesus and affirming in glass the dual nature of

Christ, which is the foundation of Christianity and the antithesis of Cathar belief that Jesus was never made flesh. Above the lineage are the Holy Spirit and God the Father.

Notre-Dame Chapel also contains a fourteenth-century statue of a smiling Mary looking down at the Infant in her arms. I don't often see statues of smiling Marys. She is usually either somber or looking exceptionally holy. Yet here in St-Nazaire I saw, in all, three smiling Marys from the fourteenth century. She looked almost giggly and girlish and more human than I have ever seen her depicted.

At the south side of the altar the Holy Cross Chapel, also dating from the thirteenth century, housed a fourteenth-century Trinity: God, with Christ before him on the cross and the Holy Ghost, in the shape of a bird, issuing from God's mouth and touching the head of Christ. A visualization of separateness and sameness. This was a depiction that Catholic and Cathar would have agreed on. Both believed in the Trinity of God.

The church organ began to sound. The first strains of a glorious Bach cantata, the gentleness before the thunder, its notes overriding the noise of the other visitors in the basilica. I sat down on one in the sea of chairs that, in neat rows, faced the altar. The cantata, written for the greater glory of God, gained momentum and swept over me. The sun lit the fiery rose window, high up on the south wall, a medieval vision of the heavenly New Jerusalem.

Below that window, mounted vertically against a wall, was the lid of the sarcophagus of one of the crusaders laid to rest in St-Nazaire, Simon de Montfort, who had shown such courage at the battle for the castellare. He would play an active role in the coming years of the Albigensian Crusade, but now his image, carved into the stone, was in repose, his hands joined in prayer. From under his feet a lion gazes up at his face. Simon wears chain mail and the mantle of the crusader, emblazoned with crosses. A scabbard cradling a long sword girdles his waist. A helmet covers his head. For eternity, he remains dressed and ready to battle for the New Jerusalem.

Even carved in stone, the image of Simon had eroded and was difficult to make out. His face had become a gentle insinuation of a nose, mouth, cheekbones. I touched the stone, feeling this remnant of a single man and inched closer to the past. There is another stone, called the siege stone, that usually rests next to Simon's sarcophagus and depicts a thirteenth-century siege. It is of great value to military historians. An inky copy of a newspaper clipping said the stone had been temporarily removed to Rome for an important exposition.

Outside the cathedral was the Éditions Loubat, the bookstore that occupied a part of the cathedral square. Judging by the number of books on the Cathars, perhaps thirty different titles, there was a modern-day resurgence in learning the other side of the story. I studied the titles and subject matter: Cathars and the Holy Grail; Cathars and Feminism; The Secret Treasure of the Cathars; What the Cathars Really Believed. Tucked between two of them was the Manual of the Inquisition by Bernard Gui, the inquisitor of Toulouse. In the revisionist twentieth century, the Cathars are considered a gentle people, noble underdogs who were the victims of brutal repression. This revisionist view seems to be mostly accurate, speculative forays into the realms of hidden treasure and the fate of the Holy Grail notwithstanding. I purchased two titles from the trim woman who ran the place. One of them was in French; I would have to read it with a dictionary by my side.

I found other echoes of the Albigensian Crusade throughout the Cité. There is a deep cistern within the tourist office in the gatehouse of the Porte Narbonnaise. It collected rainwater but of course went dry during the siege of 1209. I walked the outer walls. Patches of wild green grew in the cracks of the crenellated battlements. From the top of the parapet near the Porte d'Aude I saw the river, only a quarter of a mile away. The besieged who were dying of thirst must have been able to see it, too.

Night came and I looked out my window at the dark, round towers of the Château Comtal and the empty terrace of the Bar L'Aquarelle. I couldn't sleep and wound up making a list in my head of the 1961 graduating class of Sacred Heart School. My class. The school was four rooms on the second floor above Sacred Heart Church, two grades to a room. We numbered barely over two dozen.

I remembered most of them. Linked by eight years of the lives of the saints and daily Mass and First Holy Communion and Confirmation in the fifth grade, when we all became Soldiers of Christ, I felt that, in a way, they had all been with me, standing on the walls of the Cité overlooking the plain where the Catholic crusaders besieged the heretics.

All except Jimmy Wilson. He was the only one of us who I knew for sure was dead. Dead since Vietnam. I had seen his name, carved deep and fresh, into the black marble of the memorial wall in Washington, D.C.

Jimmy was on the other side of the parapet, gone over to Charlemagne and Raymond-Roger and Simon de Montfort. Dead eight hundred years or dead twenty-eight. They were on one side, and we, the remainder of the 1961 graduating class of Sacred Heart School, were on the other.

FIVE

The Bishops of Albi
and the Fortress of God

AT THE END OF AUGUST 1209 RAYMOND-ROGER TRENCAVEL was in prison where he would die in November. Béziers and Carcassonne were in the hands of the crusaders. It was time to choose a new viscount of Béziers from among the crusaders' ranks. The freshly appointed viscount would be required to remain in the Languedoc, secure the newly won lands, and continue the crusade against the Cathars. However, none of the greater noblemen wanted the job. The duke of Burgundy and the counts of Pol and Nevers were already turning their attention back to their holdings in the north, where fall harvest would soon begin.

Finally, Raymond-Roger's title was offered to Simon de Montfort, the hero of the first battle for the castellare. Simon accepted, but only after he elicited an oath from the other nobles that they would come to his aid if he encountered difficulties with the heretics who remained on the former Trencavel lands. And so the first secular decision of the Albigensian Crusade—who would control the lands seized in the name of God, the sort of pragmatic matter that would eventually overwhelm any religious considerations—had been made.

Why Simon de Montfort? More than demonstrating any one outstanding attribute apart from his courage in battle, Simon was a man who, by and large, fit the bill. His noble lineage could not be disputed. He was heir to the Montfort l'Amaury lordship in the Île-de-France, granted to his great-great-grandfather by Hugh Capet, king of France from 987 to 996 and founder of the Capetian dynasty, which eventually numbered fourteen kings and lasted until 1328. He had also acquitted himself bravely during the Fourth Crusade to the Holy Land.

In addition, Simon was not wealthy enough to turn down the title, unlike the greater nobles of the north. His lands in the Île-de-France were prestigious but small, and although he held the impressive English title of the earl of Leicester (through his mother), the English king had confiscated the holdings of French nobles at the conclusion of the most recent conflict between the two countries. Simon also had to provide for his wife, Alice de Montmorency, daughter of one of the oldest and noblest houses of France, and secure the future of their four sons. Simon was on a constant search for new sources of income. If personal gain could be made to coincide with religious duty, so much the better. When the crusaders elected Simon as the viscount of Béziers, he was already in his late forties, an old man by thirteenth-century standards, but still vigorous and strong. He was also ambitious, clever, shrewd, and ruthless, and he carried a hatred for the heretics that was genuine and deep. Simon truly considered himself a soldier of Christ. There is one other image of Simon, apart from that carved in his tombstone at Carcassonne, that appears high up in one of the stained glass windows of Chartres Cathedral. He is in armor, astride a prancing horse, holding lance and shield high, prepared to do holy war.

After the crusaders captured Carcassonne, large numbers of Cathars fled south to the rugged terrain of the Pyrenees. Castles and towns near the city fell to Simon like teetering dominoes. The first to surrender was Fanjeaux, several kilometers to the south of

Carcassonne. Then Castres, to the north, sent a deputation to escort Simon into the city to witness the first public burning of heretics, especially arranged for his viewing. The garrison of Mirepoix fled and the town surrendered forthwith, as did Pamiers and Saverdun in the territory of the count of Foix. Unable to raise troops, the count submitted to Simon and supplied his youngest son as hostage. Simon then marched on Albi, the last remaining town of any importance in the former Trencavel lands and an important seat of power for the Cathars. Albi offered no resistance of any kind and surrendered to him in September of 1209.

Almost no fighting took place in the districts surrounding Albi during the crusade, even though the Cathars of that region had always been strong, numerous, and organized—so much so that historians eventually dubbed the campaign launched to destroy the Cathars the Albigensian Crusade. Scholars estimate that fully one-third of the people in the precincts of Albi were either Cathars or Cathar sympathizers. I had to see the town that gave the crusade its name.

The radio in my Peugeot didn't work, so I listened to my Beatles tapes as I drove the 105-kilometer route from Carcassonne to Albi. I first headed north along the isolated D118, gently climbing along the wide, green valley of the Vallouvière, then turned to follow the snaking Dure. The road crested the Montagne Noire and spiraled down in hairpin turns and switchbacks, spilling into the town of Mazamet and the extensive plain that spread north. The small Cathar museum located in Mazamet was closed on Mondays, so I continued on to the town of Castres. From Castres I followed poplars and maples lining N112 through rolling fields and vineyards the remaining fifty kilometers to Albi. Strawberry Fields Forever.

Something was working on me. I was a little—I guess *shocked* is the word—to find that even at my leisurely pace, I had made the drive to Albi in under two hours. My mind was starting to regard medieval travel times as the norm and twentieth-century speeds as incredible. But of course they *were* incredible. Until this century people walked or rode horses and, until the railroad, traveled about as swiftly as people in the thirteenth century.

Perhaps this little shock meant that I was beginning to get a handle on the thirteenth century. At times it seemed that I wasn't understanding anything but only collecting fistfuls of facts. Peter of Castelnau murdered on the banks of the Rhône. The people of Béziers slaughtered in their cathedral. The Cathars' disbelief in Christ as human. Raymond-Roger tricked and imprisoned. Simon de Montfort's need for money.

I am a child of the twentieth century who believes in natural explanations for natural occurrences. Could I make sense of a time when the actions of spirits and demons were the cause of everyday occurrences? Too much rain. Too little rain. A goat dying. Could I truly comprehend an era when printed books were still more than 250 years in the future? When the father of the scientific method, the thirteenth-century scientist Roger Bacon, was thought to be in league with the devil by his fellow Franciscans? When the idea that blood circulated in human bodies was four hundred years away and the concept of germs more than half a millennium?

I found a pleasant café on the rue Ste-Cécile in the old quarter of Albi while it was still midmorning and dug out one of the books about the Cathars, the one in English, that I had bought in Carcassonne. Books are usually ideal companions on the road. Diversions during long nights in hotels or on the rails, shields against the noisy and boring, a retreat when sensory input overwhelms. Hardcover books are pure indulgence. Space that could be used for a sweater or more socks or—better still—left empty now holds something I am loath to abandon on a train seat or in a waiting room or atop a table in a hotel hallway.

A paperback book is a more sensible choice for the road. It can be bent to fit into the curved space behind my shaving kit and double-backed on itself for one-handed holding. Paperbacks acquired while traveling are the best to abandon. There is no smell of home lingering on their spines, and they exemplify the transitory nature of acquaintances made on the road. Picked up in Copenhagen. Left in Chamonix. Devoured for what they can give you, they are put down with a quick good-bye and rarely a lingering regret. The idea that some of them might still be somewhere on the road pleased me.

But I didn't think much of *Cathar Religion* by Michel Roquebert. It was poorly translated, sadly edited, loaded with typographical errors, and, worst of all, peppered with phrases like "One can easily accept that . . ." and "We must presuppose then . . ."

Nothing about the Cathars, or the crusaders for that matter, was coming easily to me. *Cathar Religion* abounded with the sorts of simplifications I was trying to avoid. And because I didn't like the book, I didn't want to leave it anywhere for anyone. I lugged it all through the Languedoc, and my dislike escalated to hate as its weight grew more burdensome. The only thing more hateful would have been to throw it in the trash. I lugged it back to Paris and eventually carried it home where it mocks me still from the bookcase. I closed *Cathar Religion,* buried it in the bottom of my camera bag, and walked down the rue Ste-Cécile toward the place that had drawn me to Albi.

Even after seven hundred years the Cathedral of Ste-Cécile is the tallest building in Albi. I had gleaned its dimensions and design from numerous and detailed guidebooks. But the guidebooks, dry and unimaginative, did not prepare me for the moment when I turned the last sharp corner, entered the Place Ste-Cécile, and saw the massive cathedral dwarfing all that surrounded it. Ste-Cécile loomed, straight flanks of unadorned earth-red brick rising to support the weight of the Heavenly Host. High narrow windows were interspersed close to the top. There were no flying buttresses for an enemy to scale or find shelter under during an attack. I ran my hands along the brickwork, as if stroking the hull of a huge ship. Rounded columns bulged from the cathedral's exterior walls and extended the height of the building. I stood with my back flat against the wall and looked straight up, dizzy at the height, to the horizon of red brick meeting the high blue heaven. There was a stern harmony to the cathedral, a building meant for the ages, except for the frivolous fifteenth-century porch that embellished the south entry.

Construction of the Cathedral of Ste-Cécile began in 1277 under the Catholic bishop Bernard de Castanet and took two hundred years to complete. Although the late thirteenth century was the period of High Gothic in France, the exterior of the cathedral was unapologetically Romanesque. In the aftermath of the Albigensian Crusade Ste-Cécile was designed to be a daunting fortress of God. Its twin towers had a command of the countryside. I could not capture its entirety with a camera, except from a point well beyond the Pont-Vieux that crossed the Tarn River. From that distance, perhaps two kilometers, Ste-Cécile was a battleship of God, waiting for the order to sail out and engage the enemy.

But once I was across the silly porch and inside the cathedral, the cold fortress turned into a medieval conception of the New

Jerusalem. The cathedral's interior dimensions were heroic. A ten-story building could have fit inside the arch of its single interior nave. The nave itself stretched the length of an American football field, goalpost to goalpost, from the mural of the Last Judgment on the west wall to the statue of the Virgin Mary crowning the apse behind the High Altar on the east.

The interior of Ste-Cécile also demonstrates the long, sometimes torturous affair between the Catholic Church and the state of France. In the Last Judgment mural, Charlemagne, Saint Louis, and Blanche of Castile hobnob with the apostles. The good Louis sitting in the Last Judgment gave the bishops of Albi secular power over the town in 1264, a power they enjoyed until 1789 and the French Revolution. A statue of Charlemagne guards the doorway to the choir stalls. The other niches in the choir now stand empty, but they were once occupied by statues of saints, smashed during the anticlerical zeal of the Revolution, when Ste-Cécile was temporarily transformed into a Temple of Reason.

Standing in Ste-Cécile I wished that I were a believer and secure in my beliefs. It would take a lot of the pressure off regarding questions of life after death, the nature of eternity, the ramifications of the original sin that the Catholic Church had told me was my birthright, and the power of faith to save my soul, the existence of which I would no longer question. Everything would be laid out for me, already having been figured out by Augustine and Thomas Aquinas, and transmitted to me through the nuns who taught me. But would I have to trade away my joyous doubting, my idea that human beings may just be capable of saving themselves? How much might being a believer cost me?

⚜

Albi was a seat of one of the four Cathar bishoprics in the Langue-doc. The role of the Cathar bishops was largely pastoral in nature. They were more like traveling preachers, each assisted by a *filius major* and a *filius minor,* whose roles were also pastoral.

The Cathars divided themselves into two classes, the Perfects and the Believers. Perfects had undertaken the rite of the *consola-mentum,* the gift of knowledge brought by the Holy Spirit and re-ceived through the laying on of hands. The Perfects were also referred to as *Bonne Chrétiens* or *Bonne Hommes,* perhaps in com-parison to the corrupt Catholic clergymen who then inhabited the Languedoc. Believers, those Cathars who had not yet taken the *consolamentum,* were not expected to endure the hardships re-quired of the Perfects. The Cathar bishops of Albi so freely and openly preached their beliefs that it was possible for a public de-bate to be held in 1165 between Christian and Cathar at the hilltop town of Lombers, some ten miles to the south of Albi. It was here that one Cathar was bold enough to condemn the Catholic clergy in the Languedoc as "false prophets and wolves in the midst of the Lord's flock."[5]

How did a Cathar go about gaining the spiritual realm? How did one get to heaven? A Cathar from the village of St-Paul de Fenouillet once explained to the Catholic bishop of Alet that "everything that exists under the sun and the moon is but corrup-tion and chaos."[6] As all material things—all their eyes could see, the food and water they put into their bodies, their bodies them-selves—were the product of the Devil, the only path to salvation for a Cathar was a total rejection of the physical world. This was made explicit in the *consolamentum:* "Moreover, you must hate this world and its works and all things which are of this world."[7]

The *consolamentum* relied on the First Epistle of John from the

New Testament to support this idea and the extreme asceticism that stemmed from it:

> Beloved, do not love the world, nor the things that are in this world. If anyone loves the world, there is no love for the Father in his heart. For all that is in the world is the lust of the flesh, desire of the eyes, and pride in life—things that come not from the Father but from the world. And the world and its desires shall pass away, but he who does the will of God shall endure forever. [8]

While in the ranks of the Believers, a Cathar could still marry, have sexual relations, eat meat, and generally indulge him- or herself in the material world. A Believer's sole duty was to take, on some unspecified day in the future, the *consolamentum*. If a Cathar failed to receive the rite during his or her lifetime, the spirit would be reborn into another human being (or animal—perhaps one reason the Cathars did not consume flesh) until the *consolamentum* was accomplished. Once a Believer attained the status of Perfect through the *consolamentum,* he or she was required not only to preach the doctrine to the Believers but also to set an example of how to reject the world.

The Perfects were not intermediaries between God and human beings as Catholic priests were but rather ascetic holy teachers. They denied themselves any food that was the product of sexual union, they abstained from sex, they fasted and meditated to the brink of death. Some Perfects did actually starve themselves to death in order to achieve the spiritual purity they sought. Others were more active in their pursuit of the afterlife. A female Perfect of Toulouse, one Guilelma, regularly bled herself while sitting in a hot bath and eventually poisoned herself and ate ground glass. In the eyes of the Perfect, there was no such thing as a spiritual hell. Hell was right here on earth.

In addition to the *consolamentum,* the Cathars recited the Lord's Prayer and performed the *melioramentum,* the act of bowing to a Perfect and receiving a benediction. As a result, bowing, along with refusing to swear an oath, which Cathars were forbidden to do, were signs to the crusaders of a practicing heretic.

The Cathar church welcomed peasant, merchant, and noble, a practice that appealed to my twentieth-century mind. Women participated fully in Cathar rituals. Taking the *consolamentum* usually required a successful three-year trial period for the Believer to fully appreciate what was expected of a Perfect. However, the *consolamentum* was often given on the deathbed or, as during the Albigensian Crusade, in the final hours of a siege when death was near at hand.

The Perfects were also pacifists, which raises the question of who was doing battle with Simon de Montfort's crusaders. In truth, it was mostly Christian killing Christian. Southern Catholics viewed the Albigensian Crusade as simply and solely an invasion of the south by the north and reason enough to fight. But there were strong ties between Catholic and Cathar that were undeniable. A Catholic knight of the Languedoc explained to the bishop of Toulouse why southern Catholics could not be relied upon to make war against the Cathars. "How can we? We have been brought up side by side with them. Our closest kinsmen are numbered among them. Every day we see them living worthy and honorable lives in our midst."[9]

Scholarly estimates put more than one-third of Perfects as nobly born. Bernard de Saissac, the regent who ruled in the name of Raymond-Roger Trencavel before the young viscount came of age, was an unrepentant Cathar. Esclaramonde, the sister of the count of Foix, was herself a Perfect. Lady Guirade of Lavaur was a Cathar woman renowned for her gentleness and hospitality to Cathar and Christian alike, and troubadours praised her in song.

One Christian who took a lesson from the Perfects was Saint Dominic. During his years of preaching in the Languedoc he observed that the piety, asceticism, and discipline of the Perfects were respected by the people of the Languedoc, as opposed to the disdain they held for the Catholic clergy and their practice of charging a fee for dispensing the sacraments of the church. Dominic organized his Order of Friars Preachers along lines similar to those of the Perfects. He demanded that the members of his new order be pious, self-disciplined, and educated. The order's first house was founded in 1206 in the town of Prouille, near Toulouse. Later, a convent for Cathar women who converted to Catholicism was established there. In 1216, after receiving ecclesiastical approval, the order's charter house was established in Toulouse. The Dominicans would prove worthy adversaries of the Cathars in the coming years as they eventually formed the nucleus of the Inquisition that followed hard on the heels of the Albigensian Crusade.

I could only think that it would be almost impossible to be a Perfect today. The world had spent the past seven hundred years improving materially, but making little spiritual progress. There are just too many things to forgo. In an age when cult preachers own stables of Bentleys and private jets, I was hard pressed to come up with a modern-day ascetic pacifist. I finally decided that Mohandas Gandhi came closest.

I left the cathedral and crossed the square to the Palais de la Berbie. In the *langue d'oc, Berbie* is the word for bishop. The bishop's palace was begun several years before Ste-Cécile and, like the cathedral, was built more as a fortress than as a residence. Since 1922, it has been home to more than six hundred works of Albi's most famous son, Henri de Toulouse-Lautrec. An ancestor of Lautrec's, one Baudoin, is said to have fought in the Albigensian Crusade. On whose side is unknown.

The subject of Lautrec's pictures, drawings, and famous posters, his portrayal of the Parisian demimonde at the turn of the century, is the antithesis of the "hating the world" for which the Perfects strived. Dancers dominate the most famous of his works: Jane Avril doing the can-can at the Moulin Rouge. Louis Weber contorting at the Moulin de la Galette. The faces of the audiences watching the dancers fascinated me. Hotly colored, fleshy faces, they shone with greedy lust for the pleasures of the late nineteenth century. Each room was teeming with Lautrec's images of pulsing, sensual life. I slipped on to a small circular terrace. To my left were the walls of Ste-Cécile and the meticulous garden of the palace. The sun was bright on the Tarn and automobile traffic zoomed and honked over the refurbished Pont-Vieux. Lautrec would not have made a very good Cathar.

Simon de Montfort fared poorly in his efforts to maintain control of the lands won in the summer of 1209. During the winter that followed, after most of the crusaders returned north, Simon was left with only a handful of men to keep secure the summer victories. In a letter to the pope, Simon complained of the difficulty of defending his tenuous foothold with so few men, especially in the mountainous territory of the Pyrenees. He had reason to complain. Towns that had readily pledged their allegiance to Simon at summer's end now turned against him during the cold winter months. Many knights renounced their allegiance. Peter of Aragon refused his homage, and the count of Foix openly turned against him and retook one of his castles.

Given Simon's weakened military position, it appears that the southern nobles could have, for once, united to eject him and his pitiably small force. But just as southern mores had led the nobles of the Languedoc to recant their newly pledged allegiance to Simon, so the southern trait of self-absorption in private concerns and the southerners' obsessive distrust of one another resulted in their first of many failures to join forces in the face of a common enemy. Raymond VI of Toulouse remained bent on regaining the favor of the pope at all costs. He had already turned against his nephew, Raymond-Roger Trencavel. Which southern noble would he betray next? Raymond-Roger of Foix, ever immersed in seeing to his own domain, was confident that Simon would never be able to take his main stronghold in the rugged Pyrenees. Why should he risk a battle beyond his own borders?

Simon barely held on through the long winter of 1209, and in the spring of 1210, his wife, Alice de Montmorency, led several hundred armed men from the Île-de-France to reinforce his small garrison in the Languedoc. To lead such a contingent on a long march in the Middle Ages must have required an extraordinary woman. Reinforced by Alice, Simon was able to take the military offensive. Little prepared were the nobles of the Languedoc for the terrible vengeance Simon would wreak upon them for their winter betrayals.

SIX

The Castle of Bram
and the Siege of Minerve

THE SPRING OF 1210 BROUGHT THE COMPLETION OF A CYCLE
that would be repeated throughout the early years of the Albigensian Crusade: a summer of battles and sieges, when extensive territory would be won by the crusaders, followed by a long winter of
attrition during which southern nobles would recant their allegiance to Simon, followed, in turn, by the crusaders' spring revenge. Many towns and castles in the Languedoc saw fighting
during the spring and summer of 1210, but the events at two places
in particular, the castle of Bram and the town of Minerve, typify
that deadly summer.

The town of Bram was not mentioned in my Michelin Guide
nor in any of my other guidebooks. I eventually located it after
poring over my most finely detailed Michelin map, its name in the
smallest of prints, only eighteen kilometers west of Carcassonne.
I made the drive on the N113, a well paved *route nationale,* divided
in the center by a wide swath of greenery and tall, sturdy trees.
I turned south off the N113, crossing under it, and continued down
a much smaller road, empty of traffic, over the tree-lined Canal du
Midi. Barges and houseboats, at anchor in the quiet water, lined its
banks. In another two kilometers, the narrow road crossed a single
pair of railroad tracks and I found myself in Bram. The noon hour

approached. The air was quiet, the streets spotless, and the sidewalks empty.

I spoke to the one person I saw, the woman behind the counter
of the *tabac*. I purchased a postcard, an aerial view of Bram show-
ing the perfect circular arrangement of red-roofed houses around
the fourteenth-century church, the only remaining physical evidence of the town's medieval walls. I asked the woman where I
could obtain information about the town, and she came out on the
empty sidewalk to point me in the direction of the *mairie,* the
mayor's office, which would be open for another ten minutes. At
the *mairie,* the smiling young woman behind the high wooden
counter pointed to a table that held a small stack of trifold brochures, the only tourist information available. Typed in small print
on light green paper, the brochure had the quality of a holiday
newsletter sent to relatives. Other than a fifty-word paragraph on
the last page of the brochure that talked about Simon's attack,
there were no traces left in Bram of the Albigensian Crusade. The
town walls were gone. The château was gone. Bram was now a
quiet and clean town of perhaps one or two thousand people and a
gently prosperous air. The echoes of what occurred here in 1210
had been muted, and, in a way, it was probably good that the
people of Bram did not dwell on these past events, for what did
happen here is terrible to contemplate.

Approximately one hundred knights made up the garrison of
Bram. All of them had sworn allegiance to Simon in the fall and
then, over the winter months, had recanted their solemn oaths.
With the contingent of troops led south by Alice, Simon made

short work of the poorly fortified castle, capturing it after a three-day siege. Simon straightaway hung the garrison commander. Then he ordered his crusaders to put out the eyes and hack off the noses and upper lips of the remaining knights. This was done to every single defender save one who, with the single eye that was left to him, was permitted to lead his blind and disfigured comrades from the castle of Bram to the fortress of Cabaret.

Even though the victims were fewer, Simon's revenge upon the garrison of Bram seemed more frightful than the slaughter carried out at Béziers, perhaps because I could not find even the faintest excuse for it. What was done at Bram was not carried out in the raging heat of battle. There were no mercenaries running amok. The mutilations and blindings were calculated to terrorize not only the garrison of Bram, who would be forced to live with Simon's revenge for the remainder of their lives, but anyone who laid eyes on them.

Even so, Simon had his apologists. Peter Vaux de Cernay, a chronicler of the crusade from the Île-de-France, believed that Simon acted out of military necessity at Bram. He claimed that the mutilations were a terrible but required lesson for others who might contemplate betraying their sworn allegiance to Simon. Some scholars contend that the terror visited on the garrison of Bram was the work of Arnaud Amaury, who insisted that any who resisted the crusaders pay a dreadful price, and that Simon actually preferred a more lenient course toward the southern nobles. But it appears that Simon's sadistic butchery had the opposite effect than the one intended. Instead of softening resistance, the horror inflicted on the knights at Bram stiffened the backs of the southerners against the northern crusaders. Simon was to discover this in June, when he laid siege to the fortified town of Minerve, located among the rugged hills and river gorges of the Minervois region north of Carcassonne, where a large contingent of Believers, along with more than one hundred Perfects, had found shelter.

Like Simon de Montfort, I used Carcassonne as my base. Eight hundred years after Simon's siege, Minerve remains isolated. The richness of the landscape did not change until the few final kilometers as the road began its climb toward the steep and rocky gorges formed by the Brian and Cesse rivers. At the tip of the V where the two river gorges met, towering over their dry beds and with a fine prospect of the fields and hills that stretch beyond, stood Minerve. From a distance it was difficult to discern where the rocky escarpment ended and the stone walls of the town took up the vertical climb. The gorges were perhaps 150 feet across and more than 100 feet deep, formidable barriers in any age. As I drove nearer, the fine pattern of carefully laid stone that made up the walls—the product of backbreaking human endeavor—became distinct from the underlying rock. The walls were thick and strong and followed closely the curves and angles of the rocky promontory. The gorge of the Cesse was traversed by a handsome brick bridge, the columns of its graceful supporting arches stretched downward, secured in the dry riverbed below.

I pulled into the ten-car parking lot and walked over the bridge. Although the residents could drive over the bridge—it was sufficiently wide for one car—visitors walked into the city. Minerve had an understandable, human scale to it unlike the medieval grandeur of Carcassonne. The Michelin Red Guide credited Minerve with a population of 104. Once across the gorge, I turned to the right and walked up the rue des Martyrs, eight feet wide and the main street of Minerve. The houses were constructed of either stone or rough stucco and were the same color and texture as the walls of the town. Red-tiled roofs slanted under the sun, some sprouting old-style television antennas. Unshuttered windows held curtains of delicate lace that depicted country life: young girls carrying water or boys gathering the grape harvest. My footsteps sounded alone on the rue des Martyrs. There were no flower boxes adorning the windows that faced the streets. I was suddenly reminded of St-Gilles. But this was a different kind of severity, not ugly and jarring as in St-Gilles, but natural and harmonious, born of wild isolation in the rugged hills.

At the high point of the village the rue des Martyrs widens into a tiny square, perhaps twenty feet on each side. This was the Place de la Mairie. The town's eleventh-century Romanesque church, one story with a single square tower, was on the left. The battered wooden doors were shut and barred. A small hand-lettered note tacked to them informed me that the next Mass at the church would not be celebrated for several more weeks. Adjacent to the church was a stark crucifix made of black metal, perhaps five feet in height. Across from the church was another one-story building, the office of the town's mayor. Announcements of local markets and an upcoming concert hung in its two small windows. On the third side of the square was a low wall that revealed a wide panorama of the countryside—cultivated fields among the folds of earth rising to the dark green hills scored by horizontal outcroppings of rock. I could see my Peugeot, still the only automobile in the parking lot. At one end of the wall was a stairway that led back down to the streets of the lower town and to the bridge across the gorge. Next to the stairway and in front of a palmlike plant sprouting small, bright red flowers, a thick slab of irregular stone stood upright. From its middle the shape of a dove, its wings spread in flight, had been carved out. The sunlight that shone through the carved space illuminated the silhouette of the bird in flight. The dove was a modern-day symbol of the Cathars and the sculpture Minerve's simple and elegant monument to them. Inscribed at the base in Occitan was "Als Catars" and a date, 1210. Next to the sculpture was a smaller stone engraved with the words, "Ici pour la foi cathare 180 Parfaites sont mort par les flammes." Here, for their faith, 180 Cathar Perfects were consigned to the flames.

I leaned my hands on the low wall and looked out to the line of far-off hills where earth met sky. Automobile traffic on the roads was too distant for its sound to carry to me. Here was a moment and place of peace.

The number of Perfects killed at Minerve varies according to the source. The Russian-born French scholar, Zoé Oldenbourg, who has written extensively about the Albigensian Crusade, puts the number at 140. The Michelin Guide ups the number to 180, in agreement with the monument at Minerve. Whatever the true number, Minerve was the site of the first of a number of large-scale, mass executions of Cathars during the Albigensian Crusade.

Simon knew that the most direct way to attack a castle or fortified town was to storm the gates or go over the walls using assault ladders. He also knew, however, that these methods almost never worked unless the fortification was basically weak, as at Bram, or the elements of surprise or treachery were involved. Simon had battering rams available to him. These rams consisted of a stout timber (or timbers) mounted on wheels. The whole affair was covered with a roof of tautly pulled hides that protected the men who operated the rams from arrows shot or stones hurled from above. Battering rams were sometimes able to knock a hole through a weak section of a protective wall.

Siege towers, also called belfries or, sometimes, cats, were equipped with drawbridges and had to be at least as tall as the walls they were designed to attack. Also mounted on wheels, the cat was rolled or pushed up to the walls. Within the cat were troops, crowded onto several platforms connected by stairs. When the drawbridge was dropped, the troops charged out across the drawbridge and over the walls. Cats were also covered with hides to protect those who were crammed inside from missiles and fire: made of wood, they were often set aflame by defenders after being pushed up to the ramparts. One of the best ways into a fortress was to undermine the walls by sending sappers to dig out a gallery beneath the walls, supporting it with wooden timbers. When the digging was complete the timbers were set on fire, thereby collapsing the gallery and the wall above.

However, Simon faced a unique situation at Minerve. Because of the town's position between two deep gorges, both direct assault and undermining were impossible and battering rams and cats were useless. In addition, the town had a reliable water supply from the well called the Puits-St-Rustique, named after the town's patron saint. The well was located at the base of the escarpment and the path to it from the upper town was protected by a stone gallery, as was the wellhead itself, keeping the water carriers safe from archers.

Simon was forced to rely solely on his trebuchets at Minerve. Trebuchets first appeared in the middle of the twelfth century; their long, counterweighted arms were designed to fling heavy stones in a great arc. Sometimes the stone was placed in a sling attached to the end of the long arm. The sling added distance to the shot but decreased accuracy. A trebuchet with a fifty-foot-long arm, a not uncommon length, could hurl a three-hundred-pound stone one hundred yards. To achieve such distances, the counterweight of the trebuchet had to be about 10,000 pounds. Round stones were usually the missiles of choice, as the course of their flight was slightly more predictable. Trebuchets were not able to fire with great frequency—not more than two or three times a day—and a huge amount of timber was required to build one, but they were the only weapons available to Simon that could do serious damage to the stone walls of Minerve. Smaller trebuchets could be quite accurate and manned by only a few people, but they were only effective against individual combatants like archers positioned on a wall or parapet.

Simon de Montfort had four trebuchets at his disposal at Minerve. He aimed three of them at the gates and walls of the town. The fourth trebuchet, dubbed Malevoisine, the "bad neighbor," targeted the Puits-St-Rustique. The siege dragged on for seven weeks while Simon hurled stones at Minerve with no apparent ill effect. Then, a single shot from Malevoisine made a direct hit on the well, crushing the wellhead. Rubble from its stone roof sealed the well, cutting off the town's ready access to water. Minerve's water supply was quickly depleted. Faced with the specter of the town's death from thirst, Guilhelm, the viscount of Minerve, surrendered unconditionally to Simon on 22 July 1210. However, Guilhelm did manage to extract several guarantees from the crusaders. The Catholic defenders of Minerve and the Believers, those not yet achieving the status of Perfects, were granted their freedom. Simon also promised that the life of any Perfect who recanted the Cathar doctrines would be spared. Otherwise, they faced the prospect of burning at the stake. Simon himself pleaded with a number of the Perfects to recant. The Perfects were led out of the château to a large pyre that had already been ignited and was burning fiercely. At the foot of the pyre, three of the Perfects renounced their faith and were saved from the flames but the others "remained obdurate in their wickedness, and with great gaiety of heart cast themselves into the fire."[10]

I tried the door of the mayor's office. The knob turned in my hand and I entered. Within the one-room office, a young woman sitting at a well-worn wooden desk solemnly pecked at an IBM Selectric typewriter, circa early 1960s. Wooden filing cabinets and file drawers reached floor to ceiling on three walls. They contained the records of the life of the town, fading ink on yellowing paper, for the past several hundred years. Deaths, marriages, births. In its own way, the mayor's office seemed locked into a period of time, the recent pre–computer/copier/fax age, as much a relic as the church across the tiny square.

I asked the woman if it were possible to see the interior of the church. She shook her head regretfully. "Mais, non. C'est fermé sauf pour la messe." Closed except for Mass. She smiled quickly at me, a smile that disappeared as I went out the door and she returned to her careful typing.

There was one more thing I wished to see in Minerve and that was the Puits-St-Rustique. I found a small, weathered sign nailed to a wall with an arrow indicating the route to the well. Minerve was small and I should have been able to find the Puits-St-Rustique with ease. The street, actually more a stone stairway that narrowed as I descended, ended at an arch. Behind a low wall a woman quietly tended her garden in the sun, attended by a large cat sprawled on the seat of a blue wooden chair. Beyond the arch

more stairs descended, at a steeper angle, down to the dry and
rocky river bed. I asked her the way to the well. She shaded her
eyes to get a look at me and pointed to the stairs beyond the
arch. "La."

I descended to the riverbed, passed under the arched bridge,
equally impressive from the bottom as from the top, and walked
for thirty minutes, my feet balancing on the humps of the smooth
rounded rocks, some of them as large as soccer balls, heat radiating
up from them in the stifling air of the gorge. No well. I doubled
back on a different road that climbed to the high streets of Minerve. I passed the old *léproserie*, built for the care of lepers, and the
natural bridges formed by the underflow of the Cesse, but found
no well. I passed the *candela*, the tower, slim and of crumbling
stone, that was the last remains of the thirteenth-century fortress
that saw Simon's siege. I eventually made my way back to the point
where I had started my search. I had spent an hour in hot, frustrated walking. My feet were on fire. But now there was another
person on the street, someone who would surely point me the right
way, the town's postman. He seemed incredibly busy in this slow-
moving place, bounding up flights of steps, running back down,
hopping into a Peugeot that was smaller than mine and painted
the bright yellow of the French postal service, driving twenty feet,
and hopping out again. I had to block his path to gain his attention, so single-minded was he in his task. I asked him the way to
the well. With a wave of his arm, he pointed me in the same direction I had originally started on. But at the end of the wave he
added a small movement with his hand, first downward and then
left. I must have looked puzzled, because he made the small movement with his hand again. Downward, then left.

I had missed a turn at the bottom of the stairs. I followed the
postman's hand and wound up, again, walking in the riverbed, but

this time in the other direction. The walls of Minerve loomed high to my left. After rounding a bend, I saw, high up on the right side of the gorge, a trebuchet perched above the rocks at the edge of a vineyard, ominously backlit by the sun. It looked primitively evil and efficient. I followed the direction of its sling arm and found the Puits-St-Rustique. The well sat at the base of a crumbled wall, the covered walkway that once led to it faintly discernible in a deteriorated outline, wild greenery growing in the spaces between the heaped mounds of stone. Suddenly it became clear. The trebuchet aimed at the well was a copy of old Malevoisine. Minerve let me see for myself what the siege must have been like. I had to walk to the well as the Minervois walked eight hundred years ago. I had to look up in awe at the machine of war that would destroy my last chance of resistance.

As I made my way back along the stairs and walkways the last things I noticed were a series of small, neatly lettered signs, "Défense de lancer des pierres," reminding visitors that the throwing of stones was not allowed.

SEVEN

The Lady of Lavaur and the Bishop of Toulouse

SIMON DE MONTFORT'S CRUSADERS RESTED THEIR SWORD arms during the winter of 1210–11, and the cold months passed without the clang of metal on metal. Simon was now the undisputed master over the former Trencavel domains. The Cathars had been dealt severe blows over the previous two years of fighting. Their numbers in the Languedoc had been reduced, and their Catholic sympathizers were sorely aware that continued support could result in the same fate dealt to Raymond-Roger Trencavel or the defenders of Bram. Events were, by and large, turning in favor of the crusaders, but a substantial problem still loomed for Simon and Arnaud Amaury in the figure of Raymond VI, the count of Toulouse.

Since his penance at St-Gilles, Raymond had been careful not to challenge the authority of or engage in combat with the crusaders, but the papal legate to the crusade, Arnaud Amaury, clung to the contention that the count of Toulouse still contrived to shelter and protect the Cathars, despite his reconciliation with Mother Church. A numbers of Cathars had fled the former Trencavel lands to the territories controlled by Raymond and his vassals. Arnaud Amaury and Simon believed that these heretics had to be purged from the Languedoc.

Simon had still other reasons to support an attack against the count of Toulouse. The lands now under Simon's control had, over the past two years, borne the full brunt of warfare. Castles were destroyed, fields and vineyards burned and wasted, towns torn to the ground, while the holdings of the count of Toulouse had remained unscathed. When Arnaud Amaury deemed that Raymond had to be purged of his power in order to finally root out and destroy the Cathars, Simon de Montfort could not help but agree. Simon's mouth watered at the idea of possessing Raymond's domain, and especially its crown jewel, the great city of Toulouse.

With their eyes on the lands of the count of Toulouse, Simon and Arnaud Amaury transformed the Albigensian Crusade from a holy war into a war of territorial conquest. And with this transformation the political maneuvering that had, in one way or another, accompanied the crusade since its beginning grew unabated. Simon de Montfort and Arnaud Amaury spent the long winter of 1210–11 composing letters to their pontiff in Rome, branding Raymond as a defender of heretics, attempting to convince Innocent III that the forces of the crusade must be turned against the count.

On his part, Raymond had spent the preceding two winters on the road. At the end of 1209, he had undertaken an arduous journey to Paris to reconfirm his fealty to the French king, Philip Augustus. The king received Raymond VI with suitable pomp and ceremony, but Philip Augustus was too preoccupied with his pressing problems across the English Channel to give much attention to the count's situation in the faraway Languedoc. Then, in January 1210, Raymond traveled from Paris to Rome to gain an audience with Innocent III and convince him of his fidelity to the church. Again, he was greeted cordially and treated as befitting his noble rank, but Raymond received no assurances from the pope that the crusaders would be kept from his lands.

Raymond remained in the Languedoc for a part of the winter of 1210–11, where he met face-to-face with Simon de Montfort. With the aid of Peter II, the king of Aragon, Raymond arranged two marriages in an attempt to appease Simon and to remedy the new fractures in the Languedoc. The sister of Peter of Aragon was to marry the son of Raymond VI, and Peter's son was betrothed to the daughter of Simon. The king of Aragon also ably managed a fleeting reconciliation between Simon and the ever-belligerent count of Foix.

But in the end, Raymond's attempts to divert the crusaders from his domain proved futile. In the eyes of the Catholic bishops of the Languedoc, the majority of whom were newly appointed by the pope and fired with the spirit of reform, it was undeniable that the count of Toulouse remained a Cathar sympathizer and a symbol of the general alienation of the people of the Languedoc from the Church of Rome.

On the heels of Raymond's meeting with Simon, the southern prelates sat in council at Arles. Lining up behind Arnaud Amaury, they presented Raymond VI with an ultimatum: the count must totally disarm his forces and destroy all his fortifications; he must grant Simon de Montfort unlimited entry into his lands for the purpose of driving out the heretics; finally, Raymond must undertake an overseas crusade with the promise of remaining absent from the Languedoc until granted explicit permission by the papal legate to return. If Raymond did not accept these terms, he would face the prospect of a hostile invasion by the forces of Simon de Montfort, with the blessing of the Holy Church.

Raymond found the conditions laid down by the southern bishops ridiculous and vowed that he would not comply. The king of Aragon, again a failed mediator between the crusaders and a southern noble, also viewed the terms offered to Raymond VI as

offensive and the behavior of both Simon and Arnaud Amaury as
duplicitous.

Raymond's refusal was the opportunity that Arnaud Amaury
and Simon sought. On 6 February 1211, Arnaud Amaury again excommunicated Raymond VI from the church. On 17 April 1211,
the pope confirmed the excommunication and ordered Arnaud
Amaury to seize Raymond's lands. With essentially a papal declaration of war, Simon de Montfort and his crusaders were loosed
upon the territory of the count of Toulouse.

The coming of spring brought the annual influx of summer
crusaders eager to fulfill their forty-day duty. Simon first marched
on the southern stronghold of Cabaret, where he had allowed the
blinded knights of Bram to seek refuge the previous spring. Cabaret surrendered without resistance. Simon then turned his atten-
tions to the fortified town of Lavaur, located midway between the
town of Albi and what he already coveted as his main prize,
Toulouse.

I was becoming accustomed to the lush, green fields and the regi-
mented lines of the vineyards in this land of milk and honey. I enjoyed them now in an almost proprietary way, affording them only
the most casual of glances, as if the last weeks of driving gave me a
passing ownership. My drive from Carcassonne to Lavaur proved
no different. Perhaps that was why I fell so easily for Lavaur. My
critical traveler's eye had been blinded by the beauty and peace in
the Languedoc.

Lavaur has eight thousand residents, an average size for a
town tucked into the hinterlands of southern France, away from
the booming coastline of the Mediterranean or the sprawl of a

large city. *Away* is a relative term in the Languedoc. Lavaur lies only forty-four kilometers, about twenty-six miles, east of the metropolitan center of Toulouse, the largest city in the Languedoc, but the hustle of the big city seems located at a much greater distance.

I entered Lavaur from the south, along the D112 from Carcassonne. Traffic was light at midday. I parked on a small street under shade trees, near the main north-south road through the town. A pizza place was made up to look like a Greek taverna: blue wooden chairs, bright yellow tables, light green walls hung with fishing nets. The place was two-thirds filled, the patrons either industriously eating their pizzas or lingering over their wine, relaxed, heads together in quiet conversation. A slim waitress with yellow hair clicked across the tile floor to take my order, a pizza margherita, with cheese, mushrooms, and ham, and a glass of beer.

My pizza arrived quickly—the very thin crust typical of pizza in France—and was very good. Refreshed, I settled in, happy to listen to the low, friendly buzz of people at the other tables, like the sound of distant bees carried on a summer wind, combined with the muted clink of knives and forks and glasses being set down on tabletops. A fresh breeze came through the open windows, and the line of sunlight on the red-tiled floor moved slowly and steadily across the doorway.

After lunch I nosed my Peugeot through the still-quiet streets to the east end of town. Lavaur was too small to require a map— besides, I didn't have one—but I still managed to get turned around in the oldest sections of town that lay along the western edge of a large bend in the Agout River. The streets were narrow and winding, lined with buildings of timber and red brick, marked for one-way traffic. Eventually I found a thoroughfare that rose to the upper sections of town and the heights above the river where the Cathedral of St-Alain and its grand terrace commanded views of the winding brown river and the wooded farmlands beyond.

The original church was totally destroyed in 1211 during Simon's siege. The Cathedral of St-Alain, a Romanesque affair of red brick, was built in 1254. The terrace and gardens to the north of the cathedral were once the site of a bishop's palace during the four hundred-year period beginning in the fourteenth century, when Lavaur was the seat of a bishopric.

The terrace and gardens were laid out in a complex design of shaded gravel paths and meticulously kept flower gardens that ended at a low wall on its eastern edge. The wall continued on behind the church, where I looked down over it and saw the massive courses bracing the embankment that supported the cathedral and prevented it from sliding into the river.

The terrace was largely occupied by adolescents and teenagers, clumped in twos and threes, who had come from the large school across the road to finish their two-hour lunch period. It was still a peaceful place, quiet in the noonday sun save for the buzz of youth and the real bees working the flower beds.

A notice on the cathedral wall informed me that I could take a self-guided walking tour of medieval Lavaur. All I needed to do was follow the posted signs. A five-minute walk through the quiet streets of the upper town led me to what I had come to Lavaur to see, the Esplanade du Plo, the original site of the castle of the Lady Guirade of Lavaur.

The remains of the Lady Guirade's castle had been turned into a semicircular park. The arc faced the river and ended in a low wall of sturdy stone, skillfully fitted together. The esplanade stood about one hundred feet above the waters of the Agout on the remnants of the walls of the château. Spreading shade trees were planted in neat rows, and wooden benches lined the graveled

walks. On one side of the esplanade the canopy of trees was interrupted by a sunlit court suitable for a game of *pétanque,* the French
equivalent of Italian *bocce.* There were no flower beds—unusual for
a public space in France—only clear stretches of grass between the
trees.

The esplanade was deserted except for a lone bench under the
trees occupied by a little girl and her father. I came close enough to
hear that they were playing a sing-song game. The little girl's clear
laughter was the loudest sound I had heard in Lavaur. At the end
of the esplanade, near the stone wall, out from under the trees and
in full sunlight, stood a solitary rock with, as at Minerve, the shape
of a dove carved out. The blue sky was visible through the hollow
of the dove. Birds sounded from the tops of the trees. I sat on a
bench at the edge of the trees and gazed at the sculpture and the
sunlight illuminating the dove and the immense sky that rose up
beyond the dark and low wall.

The commander of the garrison that defended Lavaur was Aimery
de Montréal, a southern knight who had twice sworn allegiance to
Simon and twice recanted. Four hundred heretics were sheltered
within the walls of the château by Guirade de Laurac, the lady of
the castle. By all accounts, Guirade was the sort of good and gentle woman that had won for the Cathars their reputation for hu-
mility, good works and generous spirit. She was well respected
throughout the Languedoc, and the troubadours praised the hospitality she accorded to all, Cathar and Catholic alike, who lodged
under her roof. At the onset of the siege of her castle, Guirade was
still numbered among the Believers and had not yet taken the *consolamentum.*

Simon began his attack in mid-April, battering the walls of Lavaur with stone missiles while his sappers dug beneath them. April became May and the stalemate continued. It was during these unsuccessful attacks that a potent ally joined Simon de Montfort and Arnaud Amaury, a hymn-writing, rabble-rousing, ex-troubadour named Folquet de Marseille, the new bishop of Toulouse.

Folquet de Marseille was born in Genoa, the son of a Genoese merchant, who at first was content to take up the family business. Then, around 1180, he began writing and singing songs of his own composition and abandoned his father's shop for the life of a wandering troubadour. He charmed the noble ladies of the Languedoc with his poems of courtly love and songs of passion.

In 1195 he abandoned the troubadour's life and entered the Cistercian monastery at Thoronet. The new monk, who combined an intensely religious calling with a gifted tongue, did not go unnoticed by the church hierarchy. In 1206, Innocent III dismissed the lazy and greedy Raymond de Rabastens and appointed Folquet de Marseille as the bishop of Toulouse. When Folquet assumed his chair at the Cathedral of St-Étienne, he found a bankrupt, dispirited, and floundering Catholic bishopric. Straightaway he began to reorganize his church and put its finances in order. He gained popular support among the citizens through the reforms he instituted and by the fiery passion of his sermons, delivered in a powerful and persuasive voice. After Innocent III raised the Albigensian Crusade Folquet established the White Brotherhood in Toulouse to enable southern Catholics to gain the same indulgences and privileges offered to the crusaders from the north. Folquet's brotherhood wore white crosses on their breasts and mostly confined themselves to terrorizing any Jews and heretics who crossed their paths within the city walls. Now, with the crusaders only a stone's throw from his city, Folquet sent five hundred volunteers from his White Brotherhood to join their ranks in attacking Lavaur. Toulousians became increasingly torn between their new bishop's exhortations against the heretics and their traditional fealty to Raymond VI. The newly formed Black Brotherhood, which Toulousians organized in direct response to Folquet's group, came to the defense of Lavaur, but to no avail.

Lavaur fell to Simon in the final days of May 1211 by a direct assault against the walls, raising the specter of treachery on the part of one of its defenders. Simon first condemned Aimery de Montréal as a traitor and then hung him from a hastily built gallows. The eighty knights of his garrison either hung with him or had their throats unceremoniously slashed after the gallows collapsed under the weight of its labors. Facing what they certainly knew to be the end of their earthly existence, the Cathars of Lavaur partook of the *consolamentum*, en masse, and were elevated to the ranks of the Perfect. The Lady Guirade was dragged from the castle and thrown down a well into which the crusaders heaped stones, crushing her to death. The remaining Perfects, some four hundred, came to their end in the blooming spring meadow outside the walls of the town, where Simon had stoked a huge funeral pyre. The burnings at Lavaur were to be the largest mass execution of heretics during the Albigensian Crusade.

A straightforward sign at the top of the three wide steps that led from the street to the esplanade explained the location and succinctly related the story of the Lady Guirade and her fellow Perfects:

haut lieu du Catharism. emplacement du château de
Dame Giraude. 1211, prise de Lavaur par S. de Montfort,
chef de la Croisade contre les Albigeois. Dame Guirade
fut jetteé dans un puits, 400 Cathares furirent dans les
flammes du plus grand bucher de la croisade.

I translated slowly. High place of Catharism. Location of the
castle of the Lady Guirade. 1211, the capture of Lavaur by Simon
de Montfort, head of the crusade against the Albigensians. The
Lady Guirade was thrown in a well, four hundred Cathars per-
ished in the flames of the largest massacre of the crusade.

There were two inscriptions on the Cathar sculpture. One of
them also referred to the events that occurred here in a matter-of-
fact way:

en ces lieux Dame Guirade et ses chevaliers affronteront
les croises de Simon de Montfort. Avril–Mai 1211.

In this place, the Lady Guirade and her knights confronted the
crusaders of Simon de Montfort, April–May 1211.

The other inscription appeared in two languages, French and
Occitan. It was the only example of the Occitan language I had
seen since Béziers:

A Lavaur, le peuple Occitan perdit son independence mais
dans sept siècles le laurier reverdira.

A Lavaur, lo poble occitan perdet son independencia. Mas
dins set segles lo laurier tornara verdejar.

These last inscriptions said that at Lavaur, the people of the
Occitan lost their independence in 1211, but after seven centuries

passed the laurel (native to the region) would bloom again. In the minds of the people of the Languedoc, the pursuit of the Cathars during the Albigensian Crusade is entwined and inseparable from the south's loss of independence and its incorporation into the kingdom of France. I recalled a piece of graffiti, rare in the south, brightly spray-painted on the side of a bus shelter between Castres and Lavaur. "Viva La Occitana," it read. I wondered, how much did the painter know of the Cathars?

The Lady Guirade, her goodness buried under stone, earned only a footnote in history by her grisly death and a brief and rather practical epitaph by Peter de Vaux Cernay, an antiheretical chronicler of the Albigensian Crusade. He wrote that her death was "a great sin and loss; for never did a living soul leave her roof without having eaten well first."[11]

In contrast to this good lady, Folquet de Marseille lived to his eightieth year, dying on Christmas Day in 1231, supposedly in the middle of composing a hymn. Forty-eight years after Folquet's death he could still be found in Dante's newly published *Paradiso.* Dante placed Folquet in the circle of heaven reserved for the poets, and described the old bishop's soul as being "like some ruby caught in the sun's full glory."[12] However, for those who remembered Folquet's calls for violence against the Cathars and his condemnation of hundreds of them to the fire, he remained the devil's bishop.

In the immediate wake of Lavaur's destruction, more towns and castles near Toulouse surrendered to Simon. At Casses, sixty more heretics were put to the stake, making a total of six hundred consigned to the flames since the burnings at Minerve. The Cathars had gone underground, no longer daring to group together and seek refuge in fortified towns or castles ruled by still-sympathetic nobles. Simon's army had grown in number during May and June of 1211, and both Arnaud Amaury and Bishop Folquet pressed him to make a direct attack on Raymond's capital city of Toulouse. Against his better military judgment, Simon mounted a siege of the city at the end of June.

Toulouse, however, proved to be neither Carcassonne nor Béziers. Its 25,000 inhabitants made Toulouse, which stretches along the north bank of the wide Garonne River, one of the largest cities in Europe. Simon could not effectively threaten the city's supplies of water or food. Nor did he have sufficient forces to attack the town's walls. His only hope was that the Catholic citizens of Toulouse, spurred on by Folquet, would open the gates of the city to him.

The population of Toulouse was evenly divided between Catholic and Cathar, but many Catholics, despite the persuasiveness of their indefatigable bishop, continued to hold a deep and abiding loyalty to the count of Toulouse and the Languedoc. They saw the crusade not as a legitimate war against heresy but as a war of conquest by the north, led by Simon de Montfort. The gates of Toulouse remained shut. After only twelve days, he broke off his attack, but Toulouse would be the focal point for the next several years of the struggle between Simon and Raymond.

I could have lingered in Lavaur. It was a pleasant town with charming streets to explore, a peaceful atmosphere, and at least one fine pizzeria, but I was aware of a growing desire, the same desire that must have once gripped Simon de Montfort: I wanted to get to Toulouse. I was only forty-four kilometers away, less than one-half hour in my twentieth-century Peugeot. I had yet to be in such a grand place on this journey, the greatest city, both then and now, in the Languedoc. I'm a city boy and had grown anxious to tread the anonymous streets of a big town. Oddly, I felt like I was sneaking into the place, beating Simon to the punch, as it were.

I left Lavaur, again on the D112, heading south and west. Now that I was craving a city, the languedocian countryside held stubbornly on, not yielding to strip malls or widened roads or heavier traffic, the outlying signs of urbanization ahead, until I passed over the loop of the Autoroute des Deux Mers, less than five kilometers from the city center, that avoids the heart of Toulouse. I crossed the Canal du Midi, here dug much wider to accommodate a city's commerce. I passed the modern sprawl of the Gare Matabiau. At the train station, the D112 became the double-barreled Allées Jean-Jaurès, inbound separated from outbound by a swath of concrete. I followed it to its terminus at the Boulevard de Strasbourg, where I spotted my hotel, the Hôtel de Paris, on the wrong, or outbound, side of the traffic-laden street. A car pulled away from the front of the hotel, and my urban instincts kicked in. A break in the oncoming traffic appeared: I pulled a fast U-turn across two lanes and slid into the newly vacated space. I hadn't caused even a small hitch in the flow of traffic. I checked in, threw my suitcase in my room, and moved the Peugeot to the underground parking lot, the entrance only ten yards ahead.

Five minutes later, I was strolling past the cool stone fountain bubbling away in the middle of the Place Wilson. Waving trees and shaded benches filled the rest of the circular plaza. Its circumference was lined with restaurants, their outdoor tables filled. One short street west of the Place Wilson was the Capitole—cultural, political, and tourist center of Toulouse. The Capitole is a vast colonnaded building, Toulouse's eighteenth-century city hall. On its east side is a square; on the west is the spacious Place du Capitole. The latter is a large expanse paved with stone and devoid of greenery. Inlaid into the stones is an Occitan cross, each of its four points embellished with three crowns. In the crowns are the twelve signs of the zodiac. Opposite the Capitole a covered arcade lined the square with cafés and ice cream shops. I found an empty table, ordered a coffee, and watched the tides of pedestrians.

The streets of Toulouse radiate from the Capitole like askew spokes of a wheel. The rue du Taur makes its bent way to the north, extending from the Capitole to the Basilica of St-Sernin, a fortress of God, like the cathedral in Albi, but hundreds of years older, surrounded by youth and bereft of statuary. The narrow rue du Taur is lined with bookstores, new and used, and take-away food stands and young students. At the corner of rue du Taur near the Capitole is a McDonald's, one of the two I found in the heart of the city. A hundred yards down another side street is the Bibliothèque Municipale.

To the west of the Capitole the rue Pargaminières leads to Les Jacobins, the founding house of the Dominicans in Toulouse and the resting place for the bones of the great Saint Thomas Aquinas. To the southwest the rue Gambetta snakes to the banks of the Garonne. The rue de Rome, part of the old *cardo maximus,* the original Roman road through Toulouse now lined with expensive shops, runs south and east to the rue de la Pomme and the Cathedral of St-Étienne, portions of which were funded and built by Raymond VI and his son.

The most obvious legacy of the Albigensian Crusade walked past my table: youth. Young people were everywhere, a direct result of the treaty that ended the crusade. The treaty established canon seats to defend against the heresy, which led to the formation of the University of Toulouse. After the smaller places I had visited, Toulouse overwhelmed the senses. There are now more than 600,000 Toulousians, and the city is the center of a booming French aerospace industry.

The Place du Capitole, near my hotel, would be my base to explore the city and navigate two nearby towns, looking for traces of the heretics and those who chased them. But for now, in the dimming evening, I sat back and relaxed and felt, inexplicably, at home. I felt sorry that Jimmy Wilson, my school friend, never got to sit in a café in Toulouse. Simon would need to bang at the door of the city for several more years, but here I sat, already in the Place du Capitole, watching its young citizens, strolling, running, alone, or arm in arm, passing my table. I was, like the veritable ton of bricks, falling hard for Toulouse.

EIGHT

Simon de Montfort at Pamiers

AFTER THE LADY GUIRADE MET HER END DOWN A WELL IN Lavaur and Simon de Montfort abandoned his siege of Toulouse, the fortunes of war seesawed back and forth between Simon and the nobles of the Languedoc for the balance of the fighting season. At first it appeared that the southern knights would finally begin to unite. Their hatred of the northern invader seemed at last to have grown stronger than their deep and historic distrust of each other. Both the counts of Foix and Comminges, whose lands lay to the south of Toulouse, pledged their military support to Raymond VI of Toulouse.

The southerners thought that their best chances for a military victory would be at Castelnaudary, which straddled the border between the domains of Raymond and Simon's holdings as the new viscount of Béziers, one-third of the distance from Carcassonne to Toulouse. Castelnaudary was pitiably fortified. With poorly built walls and no strong inner keep, it was the weakest of Simon's military outposts, and it was here in September 1211 that the southern knights attempted their first unified military action against him. The effort was folly for the south, for when Simon left Carcassonne to defend Castelnaudary, he fully displayed his audacity as a military tactician. He realized that a strong fortress not only held the besiegers at bay but also trapped those who were being attacked. If strong walls could work in both directions, weak ones could do the same, and he took advantage of the deficient fortifications at Castelnaudary. He came and went almost at will, despite the combined might of the southern nobles. From his position within the walls he dispatched emissaries, directed supply columns, and even fought pitched skirmishes against Raymond and his allies. The decisive battle took place when Raymond-Roger of Foix attempted to intercept a relief column. Simon launched a furious counterattack, and for reasons unknown the count of Toulouse failed to come to the aid of Raymond-Roger. After brief but fierce fighting, Simon was able to rescue the bulk of the relief column. It seemed the south remained unable to fight side by side on the field of battle, even in the face of their common enemy. Shortly thereafter, they raised their siege and retreated to the territories still under their control.

During the balance of the fall and throughout the winter of 1211–12, Simon's forces were once again diminished by the winter exodus of crusaders to the north, and he found himself reduced to conducting a sort of medieval hit-and-run guerrilla war. He kept his small force constantly on the move, evading attack by Raymond and striking against only smaller, weaker targets, most of which were scattered about in the lonely and rugged foothills of the Pyrenees, in the domain of Raymond-Roger of Foix. Simon was again outnumbered and lost control of many of the castles and towns he had won the previous summer. All that kept his meager force of crusaders intact that winter was his superiority as a tactician and his growing reputation as a fearsome fighter.

In the spring of 1212 Simon's army again grew into a formidable force with the arrival of the summer crusaders, and he was able to take the offensive. Methodically, he began to execute his plan to capture the area surrounding Toulouse and isolate the city; he already controlled the towns of Cahors to the north and Albi to the northeast. First, he attacked and took the city of Agen to the northwest. Then, in quick succession, the towns of Penne, Marmande, and Moissac fell. Before summer's end, in a whirlwind display of military prowess, he closed the ring around his heart's desire with the capture of the fortified towns of Muret and Auterive, both to the south of Toulouse, in the Garonne and Ariège river valleys, respectively. Simon now had a fortified presence on all the major routes in to and out of Toulouse. In full retreat, Raymond VI of Toulouse and Raymond-Roger of Foix fled across the Pyrenees to spend the coming winter in the safety of the royal court of King Peter II of Aragon. Simon, flushed by his wildly successful summer campaign, retired for the winter to the small market town of Pamiers on the Ariège, south of Toulouse, in the foothills of the Pyrennees.

I followed the N20 south from Toulouse, up the valley of the Ariège, toward the Pyrenees. The last of the city gave way to green, cultivated fields and fenced meadows interspersed with small towns. I drove through Auterive, whose capture in 1212 tied the final knot in Simon's noose around Toulouse. The outskirts of Auterive were lined with modern factories devoted, mainly, to manufacturing furniture. The N20 negotiates these shining towns by a succession of traffic circles, where road signs told me, in no uncertain terms, that I did not have the right-of-way. Past the towns the first rising slopes of the mountains made the Peugeot's engine work harder. As I approached Pamiers I had my first clear

sight of the peaks in the blue distance, many still capped with
snow while the plains below baked in the heat of early June.

It was late morning and not really hot—yet. I knew what was in
store. The morning had been cool, with a gentle breeze. Just after
noon the breeze would give way to a wind that the heat would ride
until, by 2:00 P.M., only the foolish—tourists and such—walked
the streets or stirred out of the cafés. Knowledgeable natives sat
still and talked in low voices. The wisest slept through the hottest
stretch of afternoon, behind heavy wooden shutters.

I curved off the N20 and dropped deeper into the valley of the
Ariège on the narrow, empty road that lead to Pamiers. In the distance the first dark green hills were already hazy from the advanc-
ing heat. The name on the signpost at the edge of town was in two
languages, neither of them French: Spanish and Occitan. I was in
the border area between France and Spain, and Pamiers was a border town. It was market day in the town square. With a population
of 13,000, Pamiers is the biggest town in the Ariège valley. It has
been, as long as anyone can remember, a market town. I parked
next to an octagonal fourteenth-century brick tower near the
looming Cathedral of St-Antonin and backtracked to the square.
Hot, rhythmic guitar melody above the snarled beat of drums,
noisy and sensuous, came from loudspeakers mounted on the low
buildings. The street was empty—all the action was down at the
square. I walked from one puddle of sound to the next.

I took a seat in the empty café on the square. It was late morning and the market was coming to a close. Tents and tables that
had been set up under the gnarled, venerable trees of the old
square were being noisily and efficiently disassembled and either
carted away on strong shoulders or stuffed into the backs of small
trucks. The remains of the regional produce, the riches of the

earth, that had not been sold—carrots, tomatoes, an amazing variety of greens, leeks, a rainbow of peppers, mushrooms, strong-smelling cheeses, local wine—were carefully loaded up and taken away. The noises of the market—trucks coughing to life, the scraping of boxes being dragged along the ground, the loud voices that accompany selling and buying in the open air—faded away until the square was empty except for the stragglers.

A dog yapped into the now quiet air at the far end of the square and was reprimanded by its master, a white-haired woman engaged in conversation with an even older lady sitting on a rickety wooden chair behind a table that displayed a few leeks, some tomatoes, and a sprig or two of a green herb. A cane rested against the back of the chair. Eventually, an old man came to gather up the table, the bits of produce, and the seated woman. The other woman and her dog also disappeared, and the square fell into the somnolent inactivity of the long midday hours, with people dispersed to their homes for a meal and siesta or resting quietly behind the shuttered doors of the shops that lined the square.

One more café table was occupied, by two men and a woman in business suits, probably employees of the small bank located just off the square. They ordered omelets and white wine and talked softly at their table under the awning. I called the waiter over and ordered an omelet—they looked well prepared sitting on the bankers' plates—and some white wine. He went away, and I sat in the slowly growing heat, listening to the silence of the square.

During November and December of 1212, Simon de Montfort gathered the Catholic bishops, his loyal nobles, and the leading citizens of the Languedoc at Pamiers. The purpose of the assembly was to consolidate Simon's hold upon the Languedoc and to take the first official steps to impose northern law, traditions, customs, and institutions upon the south. The results were the Statutes of Pamiers.

The statutes were designed to regulate civil matters and ignored the question of the Cathars. Although Simon still retained and marched under the crusaders' banner, he was bent on his personal crusade to become the sole master of the south. The active pursuit of the Cathars would be left to the papal legates.

At first it appeared that the statutes benefited everyone—churchmen, nobles, and common citizenry alike—except, of course, the Cathars and the still contentious southern lords. The statutes rendered to the church considerable material gain. Church property was protected, and the duties that were paid to the church, in particular the death duty, were guaranteed. The prelates themselves were exempted from the tallage, a tax paid to the local lord. In addition, they were to be held accountable to ecclesiastical authorities only. Simon rewarded his comrades from the north with the titles, castles, and fiefs of the fallen southern nobles. In return, they promised to serve Simon in any future war, not to venture across frontiers without his permission, and to be absent from the Languedoc no longer than a previously agreed upon date. For a period of twenty years, they were to have none but French knights from the north in their service, and for a period of six years, their widows and female heirs were allowed to marry no one but another northerner, save with Simon's express permission. All heirs would, from this moment forward, inherit "according to the customs and usage obtaining in Paris and that part of France surrounding."[13]

There were problems, however. With the role of the bishops minimized, the statutes left Simon to his own devices regarding the secular governance of the Langedoc. This particular point caused a deep rift between Simon and Arnaud Amaury, the former papal legate to the Albigensian Crusade and recently named archbishop of Narbonne. The archbishop viewed his new post as a reward from the pope for his service in the crusade and did not appreciate the idea of having his power diminished in any way.

The statutes also contained a series of generous measures designed to protect and improve the lot of the common people through decreased taxation and fairer treatment when they pleaded their cases in the court. But in reality these measures did little to appease the displacement and financial ruin caused by four years of an expanding, increasingly brutal war.

There is a striking architectural juxtaposition of old and new in Pamiers. At one end of the market square, opposite where the old lady had been seated at her table, is a stark and modern fountain—an arrangement of unadorned marble pyramids and cones and spheres under sheets of water that splash into the pool at its base. Across the road from the oldest structure in the town, a square thirteenth-century tower that once guarded the entrance to the city, was a modern complex of apartments, all of red brick, four stories high and balconied.

I followed the Promenade du Castella to the top of the hill that was once crowned by a medieval castle. Only some forlorn supporting walls remained. Students from the school across the street lounged on the grassy slopes. Atop the hill was an open-air space used for concerts. A temporary stage was erected at one end. Plastic soda bottles, beer bottles, and bits of paper littered the ground. Apart from the small twelfth-century doors of the darkly cool and simple Cathedral of St-Antonin, I could find no other remnants from the winter of 1213 that Simon de Montfort spent in Pamiers.

While Simon was in Pamiers busily arranging the secular affairs of the Languedoc to his liking, Innocent III in Rome was pondering whether or not the resources of the Albigensian Crusade could be better used elsewhere. The king of England had just seized most of the church's lands in his domain. The Moslems still maintained a tenacious hold on Jerusalem. The church had also just begun a crusade against the Moors in Spain.

In addition, Innocent III, over the course of several years, had dismissed the poorly educated, weak-spined, and greedy southern bishops, replacing them with educated, strong-willed men. He had in his service Folquet in Toulouse, Theodisius in Agde, and Arnaud Amaury in Narbonne. As a result, the pope had more control over religious matters in the Languedoc.

Finally, Peter II of Aragon, the current darling of the pope for his heroic victory, against stupendous odds, over the Spanish Moors at Las Navas de Tolosa, wrote to Innocent III and assured him that the Cathars in the Languedoc were no longer a problem. Reassured, the pope began to dismantle the Albigensian Crusade during the early months of 1213. In a letter to Arnaud Amaury on 15 January 1213, Innocent III referred to the Cathars in the past tense: "Foxes *were* destroying the vineyard of the lord in Provence; they have been captured. Now we must guard against a greater danger. We hear the Saracens of Spain are preparing a new army to avenge their defeat . . . moreover, the Holy Land needs assistance."[14] The pope was clear on the subject. Arnaud Amaury was to stop preaching the crusade in the Languedoc.

Innocent III also wrote Simon de Montfort and instructed him to restore to Raymond VI all the lands seized during Simon's campaigns in the territories of the count of Toulouse. Moreover, he informed Simon that the generous indulgences afforded to the crusaders in the Languedoc, including remission of all past sins for forty days of service and the right to land and booty seized during battle, from this point forward would no longer be in effect. With the pope's pronouncements, it appeared that there would be a real chance for a respite from war in the south.

But the southern nobles were not so willing to go along with the consolidation of secular power in the Languedoc by an invader from the north. Raymond and the count of Foix had passed the winter in the Aragonese court and followed closely the news from Pamiers. Despite the pope's pronouncements, they saw in the statutes drawn up by Simon the beginnings of their own end and proceeded to form alliances with the king of Aragon against him. Historically, Peter had always held considerable sway in the affairs of the Languedoc, and he was also not about to let an upstart northerner upset the balance of power in the south. Other southern nobles were soon recruited for the alliance.

This gathering of strength in the Aragonese court concerned the Catholic bishops appointed in the south. Most of them sincerely believed that ridding the Languedoc of Raymond VI was still necessary to quell the Cathars. But also in their minds were the generous privileges, as laid out at Pamiers, that would be afforded to them in a Languedoc controlled by Simon de Montfort. At their council at Lavaur in late January 1213, the prelates decided to stay the line against Raymond and those allied with him, recent letters from the pope notwithstanding. The bishops dispatched envoys to Innocent III to present their case that the Cathar heresy was alive and well in the Languedoc, despite the assurances of the king of Aragon to His Holiness. The envoys reminded the pope that Raymond had proved, on numerous occasions, an untrustworthy son of the church. Raymond needed to be driven from the Languedoc in order to purge the heresy that the Cathars still practiced, with apparent freedom, on his lands. It was Simon de Montfort, and Simon alone, through his fierce dedication to Mother Church and his unmatched military skill, who could save the Catholic Church in the Languedoc.

In May 1213, on the basis of the arguments of the persuasive envoys, Innocent III reversed his decisions. He reinstated papal indulgences to Simon and his crusaders, and he reproached Peter II of Aragon for misleading Rome on the state of affairs regarding heresy in the Languedoc. The chance for peace that was born during the winter of 1213 died in the spring, and the Albigensian Crusade, now entering its fifth summer, remained a going concern.

I had difficulty leaving Pamiers—not out of a sentimental desire to linger, but because I kept getting lost trying to get back on the road back to Toulouse. I twice wound up in a terraced residential area on the south side of town. The air was hotter than I had expected, a surprise at an altitude higher than Toulouse. The black pavement shimmered. I drove along several small streets that ended in culs-de-sac, tried to retrace my way, got turned around, and ended up back in the market square of Pamiers both times. I finally found a road going to Foix, the opposite direction from Toulouse, and intersected the N20 several kilometers south of Pamiers. I headed back north through the penetrating heat to the air-conditioned hum of my room at the Hôtel de Paris, to wait for the coming of the evening cool and a late dinner.

NINE

The Battle of Muret

THE THREATENED WITHDRAWAL OF INDULGENCES DURING the winter of 1212–13 resulted in fewer northerners undertaking the journey to the Languedoc in the spring and summer that followed. As a result, Simon's army of crusaders was smaller than in previous years. But buoyed by the thought of a Languedoc freed of northern invaders, the military forces under Raymond VI and Peter II grew significantly.

Throughout the summer of 1213 Peter II moved his troops north through the passes of the Pyrenees and along the valleys of the Ariège and the Garonne. Simon was unable to muster sufficient strength to oppose him, and the king of Aragon, with Raymond VI at his side, swept down to the fertile plains surrounding Toulouse. Peter and Raymond made a triumphant entry into the city. The citizens of Toulouse, awed by Peter's display of military might and inspired to rid the Languedoc of the northerners, rallied to his banner.

Peter, willing to bide his time, waited until September 1213 to attack his first target, the walled town of Muret at the confluence of the Louge and Garonne Rivers, nineteen kilometers south of Toulouse. Muret was defended by a handful of Simon's northern knights, perhaps thirty in all, when Peter and Raymond arrived at the city's walls, leading a contingent of more than 1,400 knights, most of them veterans of the battle against the Moors at Las Navas de Tolosa. In addition to the troops that rode with Peter and Raymond, thousands of Toulousian citizens arrived on barges towed upstream by horses from Toulouse on the Garonne. The citizens took up positions along the southern edge of the town in a natural ditch. Peter left the work of attacking the town walls to the Toulousians and massed his mounted knights on the opposite banks of the Louge, on high ground at the end of a mile-long, sloping plain to the north of Muret. Peter wanted a decisive victory, as Las Navas de Tolosa had been. He knew that Simon would have to come to the defense of the town with all of the forces he could muster, so he had chosen an excellent defensive position, with the small stream of the Saudrane River to the right of his troops and, to the left, marshy ground that was too soft and spongy to support a knight in armor on horseback. Peter's knights could not be outflanked. The only possible attack would be a near-suicidal frontal assault. On 11 September 1213, Simon and seven hundred knights, his total strength in the Languedoc, rode to the defense of Muret. His mounted troops would be outnumbered by at least two to one.

Although the Toulousians, who were preparing to lay their siege, controlled the sole bridge on the Garonne that Simon had to cross to enter Muret, the citizen army lacked not only strong leadership but also a tactical plan. When Simon and his mounted contingent rode into sight on the opposite bank of the Garonne, Toulousian nerve faltered and the citizen army retreated from the bridgehead. Simon was able to cross the bridge, enter Muret through the main gates that faced the Garonne, and join his beleaguered knights without a struggle.

I would use the nineteen-kilometer drive from Toulouse to Muret, I told myself, to regain some of my critical faculties, for I had fallen in complete love with Toulouse. I knew it for sure two hours after I hit town, sitting in a *glacerie* on the Place du Capitole in the heat of late afternoon, spooning pistachio ice cream into my mouth and gazing at the citizenry parading past my table. During the next two nights and three days I only grew more enamored, seeing Toulouse through the eyes of an idiot lover whose judgment has been burned to a crisp by the first flashes of blinding romance.

For the last two evenings in Toulouse, after dining at a progressively later hour to avoid being the first patron in whatever inevitably charming restaurant I happened across, I returned to the Place du Capitole to watch the people. My first stop was at the McDonald's at the entrance to the rue du Taur. The coffee was inexpensive and good, and although I had promised myself to take notes and pass the evening in gainful contemplation, pondering Simon and Raymond and the hunted Cathars, I only sat there, notebook and reason abandoned, my eyes on the students or map-clutching tourists, the temporary citizens of Toulouse who laughed or talked loudly or hurried along the narrow passage of sidewalk left by the sprawl of the outdoor tables.

I walked across the square and took a seat on a bench. From this vantage point, I had a good view of the guests of the old and elegant Grand Hôtel de l'Opéra who would poke their heads out from behind the hotel's wrought iron gates, testing the air. One particular couple I saw both evenings. My father would have called the man a "swell," older, handsome, the roundness of his waist diminished by fine tailoring. The woman on his arm was small-waisted, exquisite, and disdainful. The first evening they climbed into a cab headed perhaps to a late theater or some cabaret. On the second evening, they appeared briefly, then retreated behind the wrought iron and into the hotel for their fine dinner. From this voyeuristic distance they appeared eternally romantic and delightful, like rich and mysterious Jazz Age characters drawn by F. Scott Fitzgerald.

And so it went for me. It was sufficient to know that Toulouse had, in some fiercely romantic way, taken hold of me and was not letting loose. But I did know that, in the meantime, to get refocused I needed to gain some distance. A road trip to Muret would turn my mind back to the purpose of my journey.

From the Hôtel de Paris the road to Muret follows the ring of boulevards that skirt the Place du Capitole and the oldest parts of the city, then crosses the Garonne and traverses the whitewashed, worn, and quiet district of St-Cyprien before it officially leaves the city and becomes first the N20 and then the N117—four lanes filled with furious truck traffic. The road was lined with factories and outlet stores that sold leather furniture. Cavernous, aluminum-clad buildings were fed by the trucks—wood for frames, leather hides, whatever ingredients were necessary—and in turn fed back to them fine leather sofas and chairs for the four corners of the earth. On the right side of the road a mundane shopping mall's huge sign boasted sixty stores *and* indoor parking. Where Toulouse shops. This short road trip was doing its work.

The walled Muret of the thirteenth century took its triangular shape from the Louge and Garonne Rivers that bounded it, both flowing north and merging at the northern end of the town. The Allées Niel—now a pleasant commercial street one-half mile upstream from the rivers' confluence—marked the southern edge of the town. In the thirteenth century, the Allées Niel had been the deep ditch between the Louge and the Garonne where the Toulousians entrenched themselves. It served not only as part of the town's defenses but also as its garbage dump.

At the southwest corner of the triangle where the Allées Niel meets the Louge is Muret's tourist information office, a squat, modest, and modern building, filled with the icy throb of an air conditioner working overtime. The office was staffed by two women. One, behind a typewriter, was young and eager to practice her English. The other woman, older and more polished, stepped forward and became voluble when I asked about the Cathars and the thirteenth-century battle that was fought here.

"There were no Cathars here. They were all near Carcassonne or in the Pyrenees," she told me. Her voice over the drone of the air conditioner was firm. "The north wanted the land because of its richness. This was a battle of conquest. The crusade was a pretext. The battle of Muret was decisive. It was the end of the Occitan." She gathered a handful of tourist brochures for me. One contained a walking tour called the "route historique" that followed the perimeter of old Muret along the Louge and Garonne, then traversed the center of the old town to the Église St-Jacques, the church built in 1155 to replace the small chapel that had served the castle and the town since the seventh century. I also bought a booklet, in French, titled *La Bataille de Muret,* its cover a soft watercolor of a medieval fortress and a knight on horseback, for twenty-five francs.

I set out on the "route historique," descending twenty steps to the Louge, then headed north on a shaded, earthen path. On my left flowed the slow-moving green river, partly overhung by weepy trees. On my right, lining portions of the path, were the remains of the old brick-and-rock walls that had supported the castle and the medieval town. Sections of the red walls towered over my head and reached the heights of the town above. They sprouted tough vines. At the northernmost point, where the Louge mixed with the Garonne, I had to climb back up to the town in order to get around a modern bridge that blocked the path at the water's edge.

On the other side of the bridge the banks of the Garonne basked in full, hot sunlight. Here, the plain of the river was wide; perhaps one hundred feet separated the old walls from the water. Only ten feet separated the town and the Louge, but the Garonne once had deadly habits, now controlled, of wild currents and rampaging floods. The flat land between the river and the walls had been turned into a park, unoccupied except by me and a family of four that gathered under a tree next to the river. The man read. The woman appeared to sketch, looking alternately across the river at some distant point, then back to her pad of paper. The two children, a young girl of three or four and a slightly older boy, played at the river's edge.

As I walked I reflected on what these old walls had seen. The "route historique" brochure told me to be on the lookout for the remnants of the wooden bridge that the Toulousians had been unable (or unwilling) to defend. I finally stumbled upon them—the children were tossing stones at them. Three or four feet offshore a row of timbers, weathered and darkened and gnawed by time to irregular stumps, stuck up about thirty inches above the water's surface. From the arrangement of the stumps I estimated the bridge would have been about twenty feet wide, enough for Simon's seven hundred horsemen to cross three or four abreast. Over the plunking of tiny stones in the water, I could almost hear the horses' hooves shivering the bridge and driving the courage out of the Toulousians who had been charged with defending it.

Once inside the walls of Muret Simon discovered the town's dire conditions. There was less than one day's supply of food. The Toulousian citizen army at the walls made reprovisioning impossible. A siege of any length would be disastrous. He had no choice but to attack Peter's forces, massed a mile away in their marvelous defensive position on the plain.

Simon and his men passed the night in prayer and preparation. He heard Mass, conducted by Bishop Folquet, who had traveled from Toulouse with a handful of other ecclesiastics. Folquet exhorted the troops to victory. Simon divided his knights into three squadrons; one would be held in reserve and under his personal command in the event of a last-ditch effort. His orders to the mounted forces were brief and simple. They were to charge, in compact lines, across the open plain into the teeth of the southern line. They were not to expend their strength in individual combat but fight as a group.

As morning broke, Simon led his knights out of the small, secondary gate at the north end of town. They crossed the small bridge that spanned the Louge and rode out to the plain to meet the combined might of the noble lords of the Languedoc. In the camp of Peter of Aragon and the other southern nobles, dissipation, disagreement, and disarray had ruled the previous evening and continued into the morning hours. Raymond VI had urged Peter to meet Simon's attack, not with his cavalry, but with flights of arrows from the crossbow men while Simon and his men traversed the plain. Peter ridiculed Raymond's idea as cowardly. Raymond and his son, insulted, retreated to their camp in a sulk. There they remained, and they did not to take to the field the next morning. Peter then passed the eve of battle in drunken carousing.

Peter had left his knights to array themselves along the battle line as they pleased, their grooms and men at arms randomly mingled among them, resulting in gaping holes in the line. In a display of reckless bravado, Peter did not dress in his personal armor, marked with the heraldry that identified him as a king, but instead donned the armor of an ordinary knight and took a place immediately behind the first rank of the line.

Muret would prove to be that rare sort of medieval battle, the stuff of troubadours' heroic verse rather than the prolonged and filthy siege that was fought with thirst, starvation, and disease and inspired no good songs: hundreds of knights charging full tilt across an open plain toward the more poweful opponent, terrific odds to overcome, swords ringing in the air, last breaths carrying final war cries. It was, as sung by the troubadours and poets, a glorious battle. The reality was, of course, not glorious at all.

At Simon's order his first squadron charged across the plain into the heart of the Aragonese line. Peter's men were unprepared for the fury and the discipline of the attack. Simon's cavalry sliced through the center of Peter's knights, hurling them back, as one observer wrote, "like dust before a gale."[15] Then the second squadron charged, tearing the gap in the line into a gaping wound. The stamping hooves of wild-eyed horses ground the blood of gallants into the dirt, making a sticky red mud. Peter, caught in the thick of the fighting, was struck down and killed before he could identify himself to the enemy as the king of Aragon. Word of the king's death spread through the Aragonese ranks. The line broke and fled to the hills northwest of Muret, pursued by two of Simon's squadrons. In all, the cavalry battle lasted less than thirty minutes.

Back at Muret's walls, the Toulousians, unaware of Peter's death and the rout of the southern nobles, were in the midst of preparing to storm the town when Simon appeared at the head of the reserve troop. In shocked disarray, the Toulousians fled toward the river, but the mounted crusaders quickly ran them to ground and hacked them with their swords. Many Toulousians reached the Garonne, but only those few who gained the barges survived. Thousands of others drowned in the rapid river currents where they had flung themselves to escape the crusaders' swords.

After the slaughter of the poorly armed, frightened Toulousians, Simon returned to the plain to seek out Peter's remains. By the time he found the bloodied body of the thirty-six-year-old king it had already been stripped by pillagers and lay naked among the mass of moaning, soon-to-be corpses that littered the battlefield.

Guillaume le Breton, a poet from the north, described the slaughter at the walls thus:

> The men of Toulouse tried to defend themselves within their camp, but soon had to give ground. Unable to resist the furious charge they retreated shamefully before their enemies. Like a wolf who, having broken into the sheepfold by night, does not care to slake his thirst or fill his belly with meat, but is content to tear open the throats of the sheep, adding dead to the dead, lapping up blood with his tongue, so the army consecrated to God thrust through their enemies and with avenging swords executed the wrath of God on the people who offended Him doubly by deserting the faith and by associating with heretics. No one wasted time in taking booty, or prisoners, but they reddened their swords with heavy blows. . . . On that day, the power and virtue of the French shone forth clearly; they sent seventeen thousand men to the swamps of hell.[16]

The river that drowned the Toulousians now looked calm and harmless. The children's stones plunked the water, making perfect circles within circles. I turned away from the remains of the old bridge by which Simon had first led his men into Muret, and I mounted the stairway of the Quai de la Croisade to the town above. The noon hour had passed, and the heat of the afternoon had grown accordingly. I followed the rue des Cordelières, officially the oldest street in Muret, dating from 1309 when the convent of the Cordelières was an important force in Muret. The low crumbling remains of the convent lined one side of the stiflingly narrow street; above, a line of freshly laundered clothes puffed in the hot breeze. The other side was crowded with small, abused houses, their plaster cracked by the sun. At the end of the rue Cordelières, an old man and a young girl sat at a battered wooden table in front of their house. A loaf of bread sat alone on the table. Sounds of meal preparation made its way into the street. I said "Good day" as I passed. The man nodded behind weary, wary eyes. The girl stared up at me mutely.

I walked through the clean streets and stopped in the Place de la République at a café under the trees. Muret was small, only twenty thousand people in the entire town, but I had stumbled upon its liveliest place. What had been a hot wind in the sun along the Garonne was now, in the shade, a modest and refreshing breeze. I sat at an empty table among men in business suits who ate their lunch and talked, in low and serious tones, of work. My midday meal was excellent, as I had come to expect in southwestern France, a breast of chicken roasted with herbs and served with small roasted potatoes, cold beer with lunch, and fine coffee after.

I leafed through the booklet about the Battle of Muret (it now deserved capitalization). It confirmed what I had already learned: that the Cathars divided their universe into two realms, an eternally good and pure spiritual universe and an evil and decaying material world; that they had a working belief in nonviolence, abstinence, and equality of the sexes; that the Albigensian Crusade was no longer concerned about chasing the heretics but was only a pretext for conquering the Languedoc. Pretext. The same word that the woman in the tourist office used. As I read more, I realized that the booklet and her words were strikingly similar.

After I finished my coffee, I walked to the end of the Place de la République where the Église St-Jacques stood. The church, with its single spire, imitated the design of the Basilica of St-Sernin in Toulouse. If both St-Sernin and the cathedral at Albi had seemed like battleships of faith to me, St-Jacques was a much smaller vessel, snug at harbor.

I had difficulty finding the main entrance. St-Jacques had originally been built in 1156 to replace the small chapel that had become insufficient for the needs of the prospering town. In keeping with an old tradition, small brick buildings had been constructed between the chapels that radiated from the long single nave of the church. Their walls abutted without interruption. The effect was that of one continuous building with a church buried at its core. The church was dark and cool and empty. The only chapel remaining from the thirteenth century, the Chapel of the Rosary, could be entered from the main body of the church through a low and graceful archway. The chapel is small, smaller than originally built—a section of its length was sacrificed when the street outside, the rue Clément Ader, was realigned several centuries later. Exposed brick walls provided a contrast to the plastered and painted walls in the main church. A simple stone slab, perhaps three feet high and five feet long, served as the altar. The chapel was once known as the Chapel of the Agony, but was rechristened the Chapel of the Rosary after the Battle of Muret.

A simple plaque mounted on one wall tells the story:

> Dans ce sanctuaire pendant la BATAILLE de Muret
> Le 12 Septembre 1213 La Vierge Marie recommanda a
> St. Dominique de réciter et préchir La Rosaire.

None of the histories of the Battle of Muret I had read mentioned Saint Dominic, but, according to the plaque, he had accompanied Folquet of Marseille, the bishop of Toulouse, to Muret. In this sanctuary, while the battle raged less than a mile away, a vision of the Virgin Mary appeared to Dominic, calling on him to recite the Rosary and pray. On a side table in the chapel lay a prayer book and an old rosary of worn wooden beads, for use by anyone who needed them, under a simple sign that read only "Prier." Pray. I fingered the misshapen beads and ran my hands over the prayer book. Did Dominic kneel in front of this altar?

While I was in the chapel a handful of people had entered and left the church. They had knelt and bowed their head in prayer. Two of them lit candles. None stayed longer than a minute or two before they left the dark church, the hot light of the afternoon turning them into black silhouettes when they opened the church door. These simple acts of faith were as moving to me as the plaque on the chapel wall. I envied them. The church was a dark and peaceful haven. The racks of burning candles were the only lights in the dimness. Because of my Catholic youth, I was at home here. Yet, at the same time I was a stranger, not because of my faith in the rational mind of man, but because of my disbelief in the hierarchical spiritual realm that the Église St-Jacques embodied. I lingered well beyond the time my inquisitiveness about the Chapel of the Rosary had played itself out. The small church of St-Jacques comforted me, and I left it only reluctantly.

My last stop in Muret brought me back to the chilly tourist office and its two warm inhabitants. My growing suspicion proved true. The booklet on the battle of Muret had been written by the voluble woman, whose name was Simonne. She was a member of the Société des Études du Comminges, and she pulled the latest edition of the organization's publication, the *Revue de Comminges et des Pyrénées centrales,* from an oversized handbag. It was a scholarly looking journal with a gray cover. In it, Simonne had authored an article titled "Les Moulins de Muret": The Water Mills of Muret.

Simonne also told me her son worked in Cleveland at a university hospital and she once visited the United States for five weeks when she toured the south and also saw Washington, D.C., and Philadelphia. The young woman at the typewriter put on a wistful look and said she hoped to also visit the United States. Then she asked me, in slow and studied English, "Do you have a car?" I told her about my Peugeot, and she gave me a folding sunshade which advertised the sunny weather the area enjoyed. It didn't mention the heat.

Simonne said she was originally from a little village near Foix that was once Cathar. I asked her if there were any Cathars left today. She said no, shaking her head, but the people near her home were still "a little Cathar" in their outlook on life, especially when hospitality was concerned. I thought of the Lady Guirade of Lavaur and all of the smiles I had encountered in the Languedoc. I had believed it was the result of an initiative sponsored by the French government, some years ago, to try to make the French people more tourist-friendly. The initiative had apparently taken hold everywhere I'd been in this journey through the south, with the singular exception of humorless St-Gilles. But now I wondered if a lingering Cathar influence caused all these southern smiles. Did they really stem from some bureaucrat in Paris? It was certainly not small-town friendliness versus big-city coldness, as I had already basked for several days in the congenial warmth of Toulouse.

I asked Simonne about the stone obelisk mentioned in her booklet. It had been erected at the beginning of this century to commemorate the seven hundredth anniversary of the Battle of Muret and to mark the site where Peter of Aragon fell in battle all those years ago. There was a black-and-white picture of it on the final page, looking as massive and unyielding as history itself. Simonne made clicking noises with her tongue, a French way of voicing regret. Alas. The great obelisk *had* actually marked the scene of the cavalry attack where Peter II fell, and it had been originally located a little to the west of the tourist office. However, the recent construction of the four-lane highway resulted in the obelisk being relocated not once, but twice, in a rather haphazard manner. Simonne confided in me that its current location was meaningless in relation to the location of the battle. The actual site of the death of King Peter II of Aragon now lay somewhere under the concrete of the N117.

TEN

Simon de Montfort in Toulouse

SIMON'S VICTORY AT MURET STUNNED THE LANGUEDOC. HIS defeat of the combined forces of the southern lords would eventually give him control of the south and alter the course of French history, but his personal ambition to be recognized as master of the Languedoc would remain frustrated for three more long years.

The south's loss had made the fall of Toulouse inevitable, even though neither Raymond VI nor his son had directly engaged in battle and both had managed to escape the debacle unscathed. Simon was constrained from entering Toulouse until he received explicit permission from both the pope and the king of France. Because of his escalating feud with the bishop of Narbonne—the ex-crusader and former papal legate, Arnaud Amaury—Narbonne refused to accept Simon's direct rule and denied him peaceful entry. And even though the Battle of Muret eliminated forever the threat of future interference in the affairs of the Languedoc by the house of Aragon, Spain would maintain its hold on Montpellier until the year 1349, when Aragon finally sold the city to the French monarchy.

Thus, even after his decisive victory, Simon was denied entry to the three largest, richest, and most powerful cities in the Languedoc. He still did not have in his possession a suitably large southern city in the Languedoc to call his own, one where he could retire to rule his expanding domain. For the remainder of 1213 Simon was a sort of gypsy, forced to wander the region with his army in tow, from the Pyrenees to the Rhône and back, quelling the still rebellious smaller towns and strengthening his overall military position.

The Albigensian Crusade ground on through the year 1214. No grand battles were fought. No great sieges were laid. Only isolated and occasional eruptions of violence disrupted the countryside. One of these episodes concerned Baldwin, the brother of Raymond VI. A northerner in both temperament and outlook, Baldwin had lived his entire adult life in the Île-de-France, near Paris, and had served in the Albigensian Crusade under Simon de Montfort. During 1214, Baldwin was captured by mercenary knights in the service of the count of Toulouse. There were no standing orders regarding brotherly love, and Raymond's mercenaries hung Baldwin on the spot. Raymond subsequently launched a counterattack to recapture Moissac, but it fizzled and the town remained in Simon's hands.

Events in the Languedoc for the time being would be largely ignored by the greater powers in the outside world. Both Pope Innocent III and King Philip Augustus in Paris were too consumed by other concerns to give much attention to a relatively minor political matter in a far-off region. Philip Augustus was absorbed in planning still another of his seemingly endless military campaigns against the English, begun after Louis and King Richard I of England quarreled in 1191 during the Third Crusade. Louis had warred against both Richard and his brother John, who succeeded to the English throne in 1199. In Rome, the pope was already busy, to the exclusion of almost all else, preparing for the Fourth Lateran Council that was to be held during the closing months of the following year in the Lateran Palace in Rome.

The Fourth Lateran Council was destined to be ranked as one

of the greatest ecclesiastical meetings of the Middle Ages. In order to get word of the upcoming council out to the whole of Christendom, Innocent III had issued on 19 April 1213 the papal bull convoking the council, a full two and one-half years before its scheduled commencement. Four hundred and twelve bishops would descend on Rome, along with more than eight hundred abbots. Ambassadors would pour in, representing the emperor of Constantinople and the kings of France, Germany, Aragon, England, Hungary, and Portugal. Jerusalem would also send a representative, as would most of the states of Italy. Church matters surrounding events in the Languedoc would, for the time being, be left in the hands of Peter of Benvento, the newly appointed papal legate to the Languedoc.

Throughout 1214, Raymond and the other vanquished southern nobles, through the offices of Peter of Benvento, sought the mercy of the church. The count of Toulouse and the others promised, as they had done several times before, to faithfully obey the church in all matters, and it appeared to Peter of Benvento that, perhaps this time, they were in earnest. Raymond transferred the totality of his rights in the Languedoc to his son, Raymond VII, and offered to cede all of his holdings in the south to the church. As a symbol of his good faith, Raymond surrendered the keys of Toulouse to Bishop Folquet. Count Raymond-Roger of Foix gave the church custody of his castle, which Simon had been unable to capture in combat. However, the southern prelates appointed by Innocent III had excellent memories and, despite Raymond's show of contrition, were not prepared to let the new papal legate be led down the garden path. The bishops made Peter of Benvento well aware of the southern tradition of recantation, and they continued to hold fast the idea that the only solution to the problem of the Cathars lay in removing Raymond VI from the

Languedoc and supporting Simon de Montfort as the church's strongman in the south.

Early in 1215, the southern bishops held yet another council, this one in Montpellier. There, they urged Peter of Benvento to grant Simon de Montfort the city of Toulouse and all the lands thus far conquered during the crusade. The bishops finally won Peter over. He dispatched his report to the pope, agreeing with the bishops' recommendation. Innocent III took enough time away from his preparations for the upcoming Lateran Council to grant, on an interim basis, the de facto administration of Toulouse to Simon.

There was also good news for Simon from Paris. Philip Augustus had become the leading monarch in Europe after his stunning victory over the English and their allies at Bouvines in 1214. He could now turn a portion of his attention to the Languedoc. The king allowed his son, the future Louis VIII, to fulfill his crusading vows in the Languedoc. The young prince, accompanied by a large contingent of northern knights released to him by his father, arrived in April 1215. His first stop was at Narbonne, where Arnaud Amaury had refused to recognize Simon's authority in what the new bishop had come to consider *his* city. The king's son sided with Simon de Montfort and ordered Narbonne to tear down its fortifications and swear allegiance to Simon. The town quickly complied with Louis's demands. Louis and Simon then traveled to Toulouse, where Louis ordered that the Toulousians do the same. Toulouse complied also, tearing down its defenses in a matter of days.

On 15 May 1215, with both the king's son and the pope's legate at his side, Simon de Montfort triumphantly entered Toulouse. With the city that bore their family name now in the hands of

Simon de Montfort, Raymond VI and his son, the future Raymond VII, fled across the Channel to seek refuge in England.

So Simon was finally in Toulouse. This put us, Simon and me, on equal footing, and I now explored the city in a different light. I was no longer in the Toulouse of Raymond VI, defender of the Cathars, but that of Simon de Montfort, crusader extraordinaire and defender of the Catholic faith.

The day after I returned to Toulouse from Muret I visited Les Jacobins, the charter house of the Dominican Order founded by Domingo de Guzmán, the same Saint Dominic who recited the rosary in the church of St-Jacques while Simon de Montfort's knights savaged the southern forces under Peter of Aragon. After the Lateran Council officially recognized the order in November 1215, the Dominicans built their first charter house in Toulouse, establishing a presence in 1216 to counter the heretical teachings of the Cathars.

The current site of Les Jacobins is actually its third location in Toulouse. The first house of the Jacobins had been located next to the old Château Narbonnais, a dark and glum remnant of Roman times that, even in the thirteenth century, was more than a thousand years old. The thick exterior walls of the château had served as a segment of the town's outer walls. When Louis ordered the walls torn down he spared the building, and Simon de Montfort made it his headquarters, taking up residence there with his wife. Nothing of either the original Dominican charter house or the château remains. The Dominicans' second house was located somewhere on the rue de Rome, the old Roman road through

town, on the south side of the Place du Capitole. Nothing remains
of this second house, either. Although Dominic had built his first
charter house in Toulouse, the order came to be known in France
as Les Jacobins, the name deriving from a chapel dedicated to
Saint James the Great where the Dominicans had founded a com-
munity in Paris one year later, in 1217.

I had calculated that Les Jacobins would be less than a ten-
minute walk from my now-familiar haunts around Place du Capitole. I headed in the direction of the Garonne, leaving the Place du
Capitole along the tidy, narrow rue Romiguières, a commercial
street of undecorated, stern storefronts and modest banks, then
turned left for a short distance on the winding and even narrower
rue Lakanal.

Les Jacobins is prominent on all the maps distributed at the
tourist information office. It is, after all, not only the charter house
of the Dominican Order but also a profoundly beautiful example
of the southern Gothic architecture that flourished in the Languedoc in the late Middle Ages, and the final resting place of Thomas
Aquinas, the great thirteenth-century Dominican philosopher
and theologian whose influence on Western thought was profound.

The ten-minute walk stretched to twenty because I missed the
unobtrusive entrance to Les Jacobins, a narrow alley from the rue
Lakanal crowded by the noisy teenagers who attended the lycée
that stood cheek by jowl with the charter house and shared the
entryway. There is no breathtaking first view of Les Jacobins —
unlike the cathedral in Albi and the great St-Sernin right here
in Toulouse — no grand approach that revealed it in its massive
and harmonious entirety. It is tucked within the narrow streets of
the city and does not command a square. It snuck up on me, and I
first thought it was simply part of the noisy lycée that squatted
next to it.

Flocks of blackbirds soared and wheeled and squawked in the blue morning air above Les Jacobins and the equally noisy teens. I had been preoccupied with birds since the lonely town of Minerve, where I first saw the dove hollowed out and taking flight from the surrounding stone—now a twentieth-century symbol of the Cathars. I pushed through a scarred wooden door into the church. The sound of the birds and the noisy teenagers faded as the massive door swung shut behind me.

The exterior gave no hint of what lay inside. The interior seemed as enormous as heaven—enormous and graceful and at peace. The walls, the floors, the vaulted ceiling were totally bereft of statuary. The church was divided along its entire length into two long naves separated by a single center aisle of seven huge supporting pillars that rose from floor to soaring ceiling and seemed to connect heaven and earth.

A light and airy pattern was formed on the ceiling by the vaulting supported by the center pillars and the walls. It resembled a canopy of palm trees. Bands of light and dark stone decorated the columns separating the tall, slender stained glass windows that threw patches of colored light on the mosaic of the floor. The first church on the current site had been a simple rectangle of forty-five meters by twenty meters, only thirteen meters in height, and it reflected Dominic's call for simplicity in response to the Cathar's ascetic behavior. The outline of this first structure was marked by black marble slabs inlaid in the pattern of the floor. The present church, completed around 1340, also honored Dominic's call.

I had never seen a church as simple and as beautiful, one that formed such a harmonious whole, as the church of Les Jacobins. I sat down in awe on one of the plain pews in the center of the church, craning my neck in slow half-circles, left and right again, and listened to the architecture sing its own hymn of praise to God.

In front of me was the simple main altar, which held the remains of Thomas Aquinas, removed to the church in 1369, ninety-five years after his death in 1274. There is no evidence that Thomas ever resided in Toulouse. He was born in 1225 in the small town of Rosasecca, near Aquino, in Italy, and was educated first at the Benedictine monastery of Monte Cassino and then at the University of Naples. Over the objections of his nobly born mother, who did not want her son exposed to the rigors of a mendicant life, he joined the Dominicans in 1243, traveled to Paris in 1245 to continue his studies, and then followed his great teacher, Albertus Magnus, to Cologne in 1248. There, because of his physical bulk and his reluctance to speak, he was dubbed the "Dumb Ox" by fellow students, perhaps the greatest misnomer in history.

Thomas was ordained in 1250 and returned to Paris to teach in 1252. In 1259, he was summoned to Rome, where he acted as an adviser and lecturer at the papal court until his return to Paris in 1268. It was then that he entered into the medieval philosophical fray that altered the course of the Catholic Church and of philosophical thought in western Europe.

Augustine of Hippo, a former member of the Manichaeans who had subsequently converted to Christianity, had dominated Western philosophy for the previous nine hundred years. Saint Augustine had believed that human senses gave a false picture of reality and that the only path to real truth was through the divine revelations afforded to human beings through God. Only in the middle of the twelfth century, however, were the works of the Greek philosopher Aristotle translated into Latin and made available to European scholars, even though they had never been lost to Islamic thinkers. Aristotle, with his emphasis on the rational mind and his belief that all knowledge comes to human beings through the senses, as ordered and arranged by the intellect, excited the minds of Paris and began to draw supporters.

Thomas developed an elegant synthesis from the apparently antithetical approaches of Augustine and Aristotle, not only to reconcile the revealed truths of the Catholic faith with the knowledge gained from sensory experience, but also to demonstrate that revelation and reason are fully complementary and that, taken together, they allow humankind a greater and fuller picture of reality. According to Aquinas, some truths, such as that of the Incarnation of Christ, can only be known through divine revelation. Other truths, such as the composition of material objects, are known through human experience. Still other truths, such as the existence of God, can be known through both divine revelation and human reasoning, based on our experience of the world. Thomas believed that all knowledge originated in sensation and experience, but that information received through our senses can only be rendered intelligible through the power of human intellect, our ability to reason. This ability to reason, Aquinas believed, allowed human thoughts to extend to the contemplation and comprehension of the nonmaterial world, into the realities of the human soul, the realm of the angels, and the existence of God. Once attaining this level, Aquinas argued, human beings required divine revelation to understand the highest truths with which religion concerned itself.

The masterwork of Thomas Aquinas was his massive three-part, thirty-volume *Summa theologiae*. In it he poses questions and supplies answers on multiple matters of faith. The second question he asks in the *Summa* is whether or not there is a God. He puts forward five proofs for the existence of God, based on the reasoning of his mind and evidence from the material world, all in less than three pages. His second proof is typical of the five he offers, and it is my favorite because of its simplicity:

> The second way is based on the nature of causation. In the observable world causes are found to be ordered in series; we never observe, nor ever could, something causing itself, for this would mean it preceded itself, and that is not possible. Such a series of causes must however stop somewhere; for in it an earlier member causes an intermediate and the intermediate a last (whether the intermediate be one or many). Now if you eliminate a cause you also eliminate its effects, so that you cannot have a last cause, nor an intermediate one, unless you have a first. Given therefore no stop in the series of causes, and hence no first cause, there would be no intermediate causes either, and no last effect, and this would be an open mistake. One is therefore forced to suppose some first cause, to which everyone gives the name "God."[17]

It was all so straightforward for the Dumb Ox.

I had already decided to save the remainder of Les Jacobins, the cloisters, the charter house, and the Grand Refectory, for another day. Affording myself a reason to return, I promised to come back for the exhibition regarding the crusades that was currently on display in the refectory. I would have sat a little longer before the bones of Thomas, but a flock of tourists entered, scuffling their shoes and flapping their yellow jackets, making a racket more grating than the birds outside.

I went out into the sunlight and passed a group of five women with small children begging for money. They conveyed the bright and shabby glitter of Gypsies with their black hair, dark eyes, skirts, and shawls a patchwork of gaudy reds and greens and violets.

I had likened Simon de Montfort to a gypsy after the Battle of Muret, forced to wander the Languedoc because he did not have a suitably noble city to call his own. But Gypsies, with their dark yet Caucasoid features, did not reach Europe until the fourteenth or fifteenth century, when they wandered from somewhere out of the Indian subcontinent. The Gypsies have maintained their migratory life in Europe for five centuries, always on the fringes of the mainstream, relegated to the outcast's life. The mysterious and separate world they inhabit results in only occasional contact with them. The few Gypsies I've encountered usually have been women and children, in train stations or public squares or sprawled on the sidewalk, invariably asking for money. Among themselves the Gypsies speak Romany, part of the Indo-European language family. Of the seventy-five modern Indo-European languages listed in *Webster's Collegiate Dictionary,* all have verified places of origin, save Romany, whose provenience is listed as "uncertain." Even *Webster's* makes them rootless.

At first the Gypsy women were passive, holding cardboard signs with scrawled handwriting and hissing "s'il vous plait" in low repetitious voices. But I paused to stand against a wall and finish some quick notes, and in no time they were on me. One woman appeared in front of me and another on my left. Arms outstretched, hands cupped, palms up. The eternal posture of the supplicant, eternally begging for coins. Whining "s'il vous plait," they were now inches away. A third woman was about to close the last escape route on my right.

The woman on my left kissed her palm, lowered it, opened her lips, and blew her kiss to me. Pleading hands plucked and tugged at my shirt. The children were now magically huddled around my ankles and feet, limp as dead snakes. The woman who blew the kisses had a dull, washed-over invitation in her eyes. Her "s'il vous plait" was more whispered than whined. She was the youngest of the three, dark-eyed, almost pretty, her face unpocked and hair almost clean.

Her hand grazed the front pocket of my pants, coming dangerously close to the fly. Then one of her hands did brush my pants, the lightest touch. Even in this situation, even when I knew what was going on, her hand charged me with a cheap sexual electricity. It was an old Gypsy trick. The hand that touched the front of my trousers was a diversion as the others were frisking me, feeling for my money and my wallet. Before the third woman could close off my escape, I pushed away from the wall, shoving the two patting Gypsies out of my way, stepping on and over the collapsed children at my feet.

By the time I was twenty feet away, they were already swarming a man who had stopped to take a picture of his companion in front of the doors of Les Jacobins. I checked my pocket. I still had my wallet, passport, cash, camera. I checked again. Then checked a third time. I felt relief at finding I had lost nothing to the Gypsies. At the same time, I felt deep anger. The Gypsies had forcibly yanked me out of my quiet contemplation and back to the twentieth century. I was seething as I stalked away toward the river. Toulouse had handed me her first betrayal.

It took only five minutes to get from Les Jacobins to the banks of the Garonne, passing by piano stores and storefronts filled with musical instruments. I arrived at the Place Daurade on the edge of the water, still breathing heavily. Down a flight of steps a tree-lined promenade ran along the banks of the river. It was almost the lunch hour, and congestion slowed traffic to a honking crawl, allowing pedestrians to mix freely with the automobiles. I walked to the Pont-Neuf, the New Bridge, built of stone in 1542 to replace, once and for all, the old, wooden bridges that regularly washed away when the Garonne went on its rampage. Today the river is regulated by a number of dams and spillways upstream of Toulouse, and the Garonne is now placid and tame.

Men lounged in the shadows under the bridge. They had the same dark and wandering look as the women beggars who had pounced on me at Les Jacobins. Were these their men, drinking, smoking, looking surly and dangerous in the shaded recesses?

I wanted to walk, to allow my unreasoning anger to drain from me. I crossed over the stone span of the Pont-Neuf to St-Cyprien, the section of Toulouse that I had driven through on my way to Muret. I wandered unremarkable streets and, an hour later, recrossed the bridge, heading back to the heart of Toulouse. From the highest point of the arching Pont-Neuf, over the exact midpoint of the Garonne, looking toward Toulouse from where I had come, I had a superb view of Les Jacobins, austerely beautiful, a massive medieval vision in red, rising and shimmering above the line of noble trees guarding the left bank of the Garonne.

If I had been a medieval man, the proofs of Thomas Aquinas might have been enough. If I had lived in a world where the earth was the center of the universe, when mankind was the prime focus of God, when the heavens were immutable and unchanging and God's perfect realm, I may have found that ideal blending of faith and intellect, the reconciliation between the realm of the spirit and the realm of the senses, the answer to my unnamed, unadmitted desire to wed belief and knowledge.

But sitting in the simple glory of Les Jacobins at the finale of the twentieth century, I knew that the proofs of seven centuries ago were not sufficient. Thomas's first cause was today's big bang. The twentieth century and its existentialist philosophers and its advanced astronomers and quantum physicists had revealed a truer state of humankind—meaningless beings on a meaningless sphere in an indifferent universe with infinitesimally brief, almost measureless existences. We are, all of us, lonely swimmers in the midnight seas of a thousand million galaxies. All of us, rootless and wandering.

At the conclusion of his fifth proof, Aquinas had included a sentence that spun my head around:

As Augustine says, "Since God is supremely good, he would not permit any evil at all in his works, unless he were sufficiently almighty and good to bring good from evil." It is therefore a mark of the limitless goodness of God that he permits evils to exist, and draws from them good.[18]

This last line of thinking troubled me and I pondered an ageless question while I stood on the Pont-Neuf, wondering what good God had managed to draw from the slaughter at Béziers, the blindings at Bram, the burnings at Minerve and Lavaur, and all the rest of the bloody catastrophes of the Albigensian Crusade. No answer came to me. My anger was gone, replaced by a sadness, the sadness of the Gypsies, sadness at Toulouse's betrayal, the sadness of having no answers.

The slant of the late afternoon sun fired the shimmering brick of Les Jacobins to a glow that would cling to the highest reaches of the church's bell towers—and the tower of St-Sernin and of all the other spires of Toulouse, as well—long after the streets and sidewalks of the city crowded below them had retreated into the shadows of the slow summer evening.

During the summer of 1215, Simon de Montfort was primarily concerned with securing the title of count of Toulouse. Simon and his crusaders had forsaken the pursuit of heretics for a secular quest in search of land, wealth, and power. It was now fully in the hands of the Catholic Church as to who would chase the heretics in the Languedoc. The answers to the questions of Simon's title and the next pursuers of the Cathars were not forthcoming until November 1215, when Pope Innocent III opened the Fourth General Council of the Lateran in Rome, which addressed many issues. More than seventy canons concerning either church dogma or the regulation of clerics were decreed at three public sessions, held on 11, 20, and 30 November, including the call for yet another crusade to wrest the Holy Land from the infidels.

In a serious effort to polish the tarnished image of the church and bring about true reform, the council for the first time regulated a wide range of clerical activity and behavior. Priests, abbots, and bishops who were found to be living in sin were to be suspended and, if they ignored their suspensions, were to be deposed. Bishops who allowed suspended clerics to continue in their priestly duties were forever to lose their holy offices. Penalties were drafted against priests and bishops who drank and who failed to say Mass. The clergy could no longer hunt or go hawking or keep dogs or hawks. They were prohibited from taking civil employment or carrying on a trade. Clerics could not be mimes or actors, nor could they frequent taverns, except when made necessary by travel. Neither could they dice or be present at games of chance. Sober dress would henceforth be required of clerics. Their garments could be neither too long nor too short and were to be fastened at the neck. The wearing of green or red was forbidden, as was embroidery on shoes or gloves and the display of gilt on spur, saddle, bridle, or harness.

Clerics could not be part of any trial that could result in the penalty of death, be employed as soldiers, or perform surgery. Bishops could no longer accept money for absolving excommunicants, consecrating an abbey, blessing an abbot or ordaining a priest. All sacraments were to be available and dispensed free of charge. In addition to clerics, the council also regulated the dress and behavior of others groups. All Catholics had to confess at least once a year and receive the Holy Eucharist annually. All Jews and Saracens were required to wear special dress to make them easily identifiable.

In addition to strictly religious matters, Innocent III and the council did not shy away from dealing with several contested secular issues, including Simon de Montfort's claim to the territories of the count of Toulouse. The assembled prelates and Innocent himself firmly believed that the pope had the authority to replace one lord who failed to route out heresy with another who had readily shown his willingness and ability to do so. But there were problems with the business of replacing Raymond VI with Simon de Montfort as the count of Toulouse. First, Raymond continued to enjoy a modicum of clerical support, not the least of which came from Raymond's old foe, Arnaud Amaury, the bishop of Narbonne, who still smarted from Simon's current claim to the bishop's city. After all, Raymond VI had also done penance, twice, and had submitted himself wholly to the church. Second, even if Raymond VI did deserve the loss of his title and lands, his son and heir, Raymond VII, certainly had done nothing in the eyes of the church to deserve such a fate. After lengthy debate, mostly in private session, the pope, with the approval of the council, arrived at a resolution. He granted all of the conquered lands of Raymond VI to Simon de Montfort. Raymond VI was granted a pension of four hundred marks per year, and the remainder of the lands that he had not lost to Simon were placed under the guardianship of the church until Raymond's son came of age. As proclaimed by the Lateran Council, Simon de Montfort was now the rightful count of Toulouse, viscount of Narbonne, and viscount of Béziers and Carcassonne.

Innocent III and the council also addressed important matters of dogma, many of them in direct response to the dualist Cathar heresy. The very first canon drawn up by the council decreed a statement of belief. The canon held that there was only one true God, one creator of all things, and that Christ was both truly God and truly man. In eternity there is a reward for the good and punishment for the unrepentant sinner. This canon also made explicit, for the very first time, that "Transubstantiatis pane in corpus et vino in sanguinem," the revealed Catholic truth that bread and wine, when consecrated during the Mass, are transubstantiated into the Body and Blood of Christ, and that only an ordained priest can bring about this change.

The third canon dealt directly with the practical matters of the pursuit, exposure, and punishment of heretics. Most insidiously, the church did not have to prove anyone to be a heretic. Rather, the church needed only to accuse, and those accused were required to prove their innocence. Failure to prove one's innocence resulted first in excommunication from the church. Twelve continuous months of excommunication resulted in final condemnation as a heretic. However, as the Fourth Lateran Council had also forbidden clergymen to assist in any trial that could result in a sentence of death being imposed, all professed or convicted heretics were to be turned over to secular authorities for "suitable" punishment. Suitable punishment for heresy was, of course, burning at the stake. Ironically, the burning of heretics was first described as fitting punishment in a legal text written in 1197 by none other than King Peter II of Aragon.

Princes and nobles of lower rank were admonished to swear, under threat of excommunication or church interdict, that they would banish all whom the church pointed to as heretics. This oath was to be sworn by the princes upon assuming their titles. If a prince failed to so swear within a year, the pope was free to release the prince's vassals from their suzerainty and to offer the prince's territories to any Catholic nobleman who would drive out the heretics. Catholics who took up arms against any heretical sect were granted the same privileges as those who fought in the Holy Land.

All supporters and sympathizers of heretics were to be excommunicated. Bishops were now required to visit at least yearly any place where even the rumor of heresy existed and to take sworn testimony of witnesses in good standing with the church. If necessary, the entire population of a region could be placed under oath. Those who had knowledge of heretics, or of any who differed in life or manners in general from the known faithful, were required to report such information to the visiting bishop. Refusal to take the oath given by the bishop was in itself a presumption of heresy. To ensure that this course would be stayed, annual ecclesiastical meetings were to be held to reinforce these procedures.

By the spring of 1216 it was evident that Cathars, who had become a distant consideration in the struggle for the control of the Languedoc, would now be subject to the scrutiny of the formal mechanism put in place by the Fourth Lateran Council and Pope Innocent III. No great defender remained for the Cathars. They could now be chased down efficiently. In two decades, when the measures instituted by Innocent III at the Fourth Lateran Council would be used by another pope as the blueprint for the notorious Papal Inquisition, it would be the job of the educated and disciplined members of the Dominican Order to do the hunting. But for the time being, that job of chasing heretics would be put into the hands of the local bishops.

These matters concerning the heretics were now of no concern to Simon de Montfort. The important thing was that he had been recognized by the pope as the legitimate count of Toulouse. In April of 1216, he journeyed to Paris to pay homage to the king of France. Philip Augustus also confirmed and recognized Simon's string of new titles. As spring warmth spread toward Toulouse, Simon de Montfort, a Frenchman from the Île-de-France, far to the north, had reached the height of his power in the south and was now the undisputed master of the Languedoc. Poor Simon had no idea how brief his finest spring would be.

ELEVEN

The Siege of Beaucaire and the Return of the Raymonds

SIMON'S RISING STAR BEGAN TO BE ECLIPSED AT PRECISELY the moment it reached its zenith. As always, discontent rumbled just below the seemingly settled surface of the Languedoc. The citizens of Toulouse considered Simon an occupier and the Languedoc a conquered country. Many Toulousians still burned with the memory of their fathers, sons, and husbands who were slaughtered or drowned in the swift currents of the Garonne in the aftermath of Muret. They harbored a covert hostility that awaited only the proper opportunity to rear up and exhibit itself. The other large cosmopolitan cities of the south, rich in their own culture and traditions, particularly resented the influx of and domination by the northern French, whom they considered uncultured and uncouth. After Simon's investiture as count of Toulouse, the French royal family in Paris refocused their attention on England, and fewer northerners were interested in making the journey south, either to fight or to settle, after Simon occupied Toulouse. With fewer men and scant attention from the king, Simon was not as secure militarily as he seemed.

In 1216, Pope Innocent III, the indefatigable hunter of heretics, died in the town of Perugia while on a journey to northern Italy. His successor, Honorius III, was already an old man when he ascended to the papacy, and the concerns of the Languedoc took a

distant second to his preoccupation with the Fifth Crusade, which
was about to be launched to the Holy Land, as decreed by the
Fourth Lateran Council. In any event, Honorius was a cautious
man who, except for the Fifth Crusade, vastly preferred nego-
tiation to confrontation. The southern bishops appointed by Innocent III, once zealous in supporting Simon and rooting out
the Cathars, now directed their energies to protecting the rights
and properties of their own churches in the wake of Innocent's
demise.

It was in April 1216, while Simon was paying homage to Philip
Augustus in Paris, that Raymond VI and his son quietly took ship
from England and sailed for the Mediterranean port of Marseilles
in Provence. After landfall, Raymond VI made his way westward,
along the coastline and over the Pyrenees to the kingdom of
Aragon, to raise an army to regain Toulouse. His son remained behind in Provence, then still part of the Holy Roman Empire and
beyond Simon's official reach, to rally support for his father's cause.

That support was swift in coming. The cities along the lower
Rhône River that had fallen under Simon's rule resented the reign
of the new count of Toulouse. In particular, the fortified town of
Beaucaire was eager to turn its back on Simon. It was to Beaucaire's castle that the assassin of Peter of Castelnau had fled. The
town had been a part of Provence held by the bishop of Arles, but
in 1215 the bishop had presented it as a fief to Simon in recognition
of his crusading efforts in the Languedoc. Beaucaire had a long
connection with the house of Toulouse. The town had been the
scene of an extravagant court held by Raymond V of Toulouse in
1174 during which he allegedly scattered gold coins into the fields
and directed the farmers to plow them under. It had also become
the site of one of the most famous of all the medieval fairs, when
thousands would flock to the town each July to trade, drink, and be

entertained. The citizens had made it known that they would embrace the return of the legitimate count of Toulouse.

In May of 1216 Raymond VII led a quickly raised contingent of local troops across the Rhône and entered the town. The townspeople greeted the young Raymond with wild enthusiasm and joined in the pursuit of Simon de Montfort's small garrison—consisting mainly of Frenchmen from the north—out of the town proper and into the fortified, triangular tower, the *redorte*, that lay immediately north of the town walls. Simon's troops were soon forced to retreat from the *redorte* and withdraw into the castle situated above the town on the rocky heights along the river's edge. Raymond's forces quickly erected a temporary wall stretching from the town to the *redorte*, hemming in the castle and cutting off Simon's men. Young Raymond called for their surrender, and, with their backs up against the Rhône and Raymond's men encircling them, the situation for them seemed hopeless. But the isolated garrison rebuffed Raymond's call for surrender and valiantly resisted his attacks throughout May and June.

When a messenger from Beaucaire arrived in Toulouse with news of the attack, Simon immediately departed for the scene of battle, gathering troops along the route. He arrived at the walls of Beaucaire in mid-June and quickly surrounded the town and the temporary fortifications erected by Raymond. Throughout the summer a strange double siege ensued. Simon's garrison was trapped by young Raymond, who held the town. Outside the town, Raymond was, in turn, surrounded by Simon and his forces.

Raymond VII continued his attacks on the château. Simon attempted to sever Raymond's supply lines and lure him into open battle outside the city walls. Both Simon and Raymond were unsuccessful. As starvation finally began to take its toll on the troops in the château, who had been reduced to eating their horses,

Simon, in final desperation, launched three direct assaults on the walls of Beaucaire, but to no avail. On 24 August 1216, Simon lifted his siege and abandoned Beaucaire and its fortifications to Raymond VII in return for the safe release of his ragged, starving troops.

When I began my journey in Arles, vainly searching for the exact spot where the Cistercian monk, Peter of Castelnau, was murdered, I had approached Beaucaire from the south, along the flat and winding river road from Arles, the same route that the murderer had followed when he fled to seek shelter. Now I came at it from the west, the direction from which Simon would have come. I was back in the green northern edge of the great Camargue, back where I had started my journey. The weather had worsened. The air was cool and damp, the skies held ominous clouds, and a smoky fog rose from the earth, blurring the silhouettes of trees and hedgerows into looming shapes.

I neared the town on the D38, a narrow ribbon, sometimes running straight along the crisscross of canals, sometimes arcing in a long curve through the plains. For the entire distance east of St-Gilles, which I passed quickly, the road was empty of other traffic. The D38 had no shoulders, and on both sides of the road, at its very edge, the earth plunged off in deep ditches. I hoped I did not meet anyone traveling in the opposite direction. The fog added to my sense of isolation.

The first vision of Beaucaire in the fog-strange and shadowed distance was an outline of black shapes against the sky—a mass of towers and turrets and parapets and irregular structures sticking up into the air, all joined by a low wall. Abetted by the fog, I mistook

the gloomy silhouette for Beaucaire's castle—the castle that Simon
and Raymond VII battled over—but as I came closer the shadows
revealed a dusty, deserted cement factory.

I found a sea of empty parking spaces along the quay of the
Canal du Rhône à Sète, where a few unmoving old men and one
weathered woman occupied benches. The water was filled with
empty pleasure boats and barges at anchor. Barge cruises along the
canals west of the Rhône and throughout the Languedoc were big
business. The old boats had been scraped down and painted in
shining yellows or bright reds or deep blues and converted into
floating hotels, fitted with flowerpots and deck chairs.

On a normal day, this would have been the prettiest, perhaps
the liveliest, part of Beaucaire, with market stalls operating, but I
had arrived on a gloomy and empty Monday morning, the final
day of a four-day religious holiday that halted all commercial and
social activity. The streets were empty except for stacked bags of
garbage and piles of unremoved dog shit. I could not tell if this ac-
cumulation of filth was due to the holiday or was the normal situation. Because some life must be sustained, one or two *boulangeries*
and a *charcuterie* were open, but I noticed that these few places
were run by people who had the same sullen look as the people of
St-Gilles. The cafés and bars were filled with men standing at the
bar, necks craned to the mounted televisions tuned to the soccer
matches.

Even though the castle of Beaucaire is largely a ruin, it remains
the primary attraction of the town huddled below it. I made my
way on foot through the neglected streets toward the outcropping
of high rock and the castle that still dominated the city, and soon
I arrived at the empty Place du Château. At one end of the square
a flight of crumbling stone steps ended in a pair of tall wrought
iron gates. The gates were hung with faded advertisements for the

eagle show, an event held every afternoon and evening when eagles were loosed from the abandoned terraces to soar above the castle and over the flat plain and the river below.

I pushed at the iron gates. They were held firmly closed with a huge rusting padlock. I was shut out. I peered between the iron bars. The castle had been reduced to a grassy ruin, with a few tumbled stones and large triangular tower. From this tower there are supposed to be breathtaking views of the Rhône valley and of Tarascon, Beaucaire's sister city across the river, and that town's well-preserved castle. I could imagine tourists strolling casually in the grass, snapping photographs, but today it was as inaccessible to me as it had been to Raymond VII when he besieged Simon's crusaders within.

If I could not gain entry to what remained of the castle proper, I consoled myself with the idea that I could view the castle as a besieger and that, in fact, the best place to see it in its massive entirety, to imagine its former strength, would be from the bottom looking up. I abandoned the stairs and instead walked the perimeter. It took me twenty minutes to circumnavigate the base of the rock upon which the castle stood. The place certainly looked impregnable to me. Sapping and undermining the walls would have been impossible, like trying to collapse the Rock of Gibraltar. From the flats between the castle and the river I surveyed sheer cliffs that rose 150 feet. Atop the cliffs stood another 100 feet of castle wall. The side facing the river was the most forbidding, but the other sides were also well fortified, and I could easily imagine that, in the days before artillery and cannon, fifty good men, with enough food and water and the grace of God to keep them from disease, could hold the place forever.

In the thirteenth century, the flats would have been located somewhere in the flowing water of the Rhône, but the river had since changed course, curving away from the rock that supports the castle, and now lies several hundred yards to the east. The flats are divided into parking lots, dirt *pétanque* courts, and, quite oddly I thought, a full-length American-style basketball court. They were largely empty this holiday Monday—only one *pétanque* court was in use for a contest that had drawn a small group of subdued observers.

In St-Gilles, something had whispered in my ear, "Cut and run." The place wasn't right for me. The same whisper came to me again in Beaucaire. Castle closed. Dog shit and garbage. No restaurants. No banks to change money. Raymond VII outlasted Simon de Montfort at Beaucaire. The empty Monday had outlasted me. I quickened my pace back to the lonely parking lot, fired up the Peugeot, and headed to the Autoroute Languedocienne, running west, back to the joys of Toulouse.

News of the stalemate between Simon and the young Raymond at Beaucaire, along with word of the troop-raising activities by Raymond VI in Aragon, reached Toulouse, where a number of citizens had managed to maintain contact with their former count. The siege of Beaucaire was the first military engagement since the beginning of the Albigensian Crusade, seven years prior, from which Simon did not emerge the clear victor. He persuaded himself that the root cause of his failure lay in the treachery being hatched against him by the Toulousians. He would make them pay dearly.

Simon immediately departed Beaucaire and the Rhône valley and traveled the breadth of the Languedoc in a remarkable four days, arriving at the gates of Toulouse on 28 August. There he was met by a delegation of prominent citizens whom he promptly tossed into the cellars of his headquarters at the gloomy Château Narbonnais. Simon then dispatched his crusaders in small raiding parties to plunder the richest houses. Rioting broke out when the Toulousians learned of the looting, and the riots soon escalated to full-scale rebellion. A number of Simon's raiders became trapped in isolated corners of the city, holding off angry mobs of citizens. After an entire day of street fighting Simon called for a meeting with the Toulousians at Villeneuve, a small suburb. Simon offered safe conduct and amnesty to all those who attended, save those identified as the ringleaders. Reassured of Simon's word of amnesty by Bishop Folquet, several hundred citizens traveled to Villeneuve.

The parlay began, on condition of the release of Simon's crusaders trapped in Toulouse. No sooner were Simon's crusaders freed than he seized all the citizens to whom he had offered safe conduct and herded them, en masse, into the bowels of the Château Narbonnais to join their languishing companions.

Simon's crusaders now occupied Toulouse in force. The four hundred prisoners that Simon had gathered were dispersed throughout the castles under Simon's control in the Languedoc, as surety for the city's cooperation in the future. Simon destroyed whatever fortified walls still stood and demanded that the city pay him reparations in the enormous sum of thirty thousand marks. The citizens of Toulouse paid this price, but, despite the onerous fine, the total destruction of their city walls, and the incarceration of their finest numbers, their southern spirit was not subdued, and the fires of hate toward Simon de Montfort burned hotter and higher than ever before.

TWELVE

The Ladies of Toulouse

SIMON'S FOUR-DAY MARCH TOOK ME SLIGHTLY MORE THAN four hours on the Autoroute Languedocienne. I arrived late in the afternoon but still a few hours before the sun would fire the spires of the city to a glowing red. I replaced the Peugeot in the underground parking lot of the Allées Jean-Jaurès, threw my camera bag into my room at the Hôtel de Paris, chatted vacuously with the desk clerk, and walked the animated, noisy streets of this happy city north along the Boulevard Strasbourg lined with fancy shops and discreet, almost unrecognizable jewelry stores, then along the Boulevard D'Arcole. People filled the sidewalk and spilled out onto the street as they collected around low, long tables piled with shirts and sweaters and aluminum cooking pots and colorful scarves.

I proceeded down the narrow, high-walled rue St-Bernard and once more took in the breadth of the Basilica of St-Sernin. St-Sernin was and is the largest Romanesque church in all of western Europe. Because construction of the present St-Sernin began in the tenth century, it does not soar like the later Gothic churches and is only sixty-eight feet from the floor to the highest vaults of the roof. But the basilica was designed as a stopping place for the hordes of pilgrims on the holy route to Santiago de Compostela in Spain. The interior dimensions of the church are awesome: 377 feet long, 210 feet wide—large enough to hold two American football fields side by side. It required four centuries to complete the basilica, and in 1855 St-Sernin was restored by the omnipresent restorer of French medieval buildings, Viollet-le-Duc. Entry to the southern transept is through the ancient Porte des Comtes—the Doorway of the Counts—so named because to the left of the doorway is an alcove that contains sarcophagi of three of the counts of Toulouse. I stared at them through the dimness and the metal grillwork that sealed the alcove. I could not determine which counts of Toulouse were lying there. I only knew that Raymond VI was not among them.

The radiating chapels at the north end are the grandest part of the basilica and also the oldest. They support the five-tiered bell tower, which resembles a fanciful stone wedding cake. The three lower tiers were built in the twelfth century, and the two upper stories were only added 150 years later. St-Sernin, a harmonious whole, pleased my eye. It was surrounded by youth, walking and laughing or conversing intensely on the benches that lined the sidewalks around the building.

I made my way south again, poking along the rue du Taur, pausing in front of dusty book shops, inspecting glass-fronted cases in small stores filled with the French version of fast food: long, crusty baguettes, sliced lengthwise and topped with cheese and butter, or thinly shaved slices of ham; delicate tarts topped with sliced kiwi and strawberries; tremendous chocolate-filled croissants that made my head swim with their sweet and delicate aroma.

I walked past the sixteenth-century *donjon*, also restored by Viollet-le-Duc and now the main tourist office, and once more found myself at the center of Toulouse and my favorite haunt, the Place du Capitole. For the length of my walk the life of Toulouse, this town that Raymond and Simon had fought over so bitterly more than seven centuries ago, had swirled by me, pulling me, and I felt joyously captured and carried along in its clamorous, dynamic rush.

In the summer of 1217 Simon de Montfort once again left Toulouse marching east, crossing over the Rhône and entering Provence, straight into the realm of the Holy Roman Empire, bent on punishing those nobles who had aided Raymond VII at Beaucaire the year before. With Simon away, the citizens of Toulouse dispatched a messenger to Raymond VI, actively engaged in raising an army in Aragon. If Raymond brought with him sufficient forces to defend Toulouse against Simon's return, the citizens would give Toulouse over to Raymond and rise up against the garrison that Simon had left behind to hold the city.

It was an offer Raymond VI could not ignore. The time was right, and the displaced count lost no time. He crossed the Pyrenees and was joined by the counts of Foix and Comminges and numerous other mountain barons. Raymond's growing army traveled north, staying in the smaller valleys, moving with such stealth that he was within twenty-five miles of Toulouse before the alarm was raised. His troops met only minor resistance from small outposts and, on 13 September 1217, Raymond entered Toulouse. It was only the joyous noise of the citizens welcoming Raymond that alerted the garrison in the Château Narbonnais that something was amiss in their city. Alice de Montmorency, Simon's wife, wondered aloud who the rabble were that caused such an uproar. "Alas, yesterday everything was going so well,"[19] she was reported to have said when told that Raymond VI had returned to Toulouse, riding at the head of an occupying army.

Raymond VI did not attempt an attack in earnest, nor did he try to occupy the château, which provided refuge for Alice, for the garrison, and for the garrulous Bishop Folquet. Instead, he recruited the ecstatic citizens of Toulouse to rebuild the city's defenses and fortifications. Everyone worked with a wild frenzy—the men dug ditches, hauled rubble, manned the watchtowers, rebuilt walls; the ladies, both noble and common, were trained in the operation of the trebuchet.

The Château Narbonnais had been designed to repel attacks on Toulouse from its southern flank, where it presented a forbidding, blank stone face. However, the northern wall, which faced the city, was decorated with windows and open galleries on its floors and was exposed to citizens of the town. The women of Toulouse honed their skills on the trebuchet by hurling projectiles at the windows and galleries. Few of their missiles actually struck home, but one stone did hit true during a Mass in the chapel, and a chunk of dislodged masonry killed one of the attending prelates.

While Toulousians refortified their city, Alice, trapped within the château, urgently dispatched a messenger to Simon, still chasing about on the east side of the Rhône. Perhaps Simon did not fully grasp the desperation of those in the château described by his wife's messenger. In any event, Simon took his time, remaining to parley with some of the Provençal nobles, and did not return to Toulouse until mid-October.

When Simon did return, he found a city that had been greatly refortified in his absence. Raymond's crossbowmen manned the three-tiered tower of the Basilica of St-Sernin and were perched in the spires of other churches. A large food supply had been set in and still more goods were entering Toulouse by way of the two bridges that crossed the Garonne from the town of St-Cyprien, the district I had found so nondescript. Despite the number of Toulousians still held hostage by Simon in his castles throughout the Languedoc, the morale of the remaining citizens of Toulouse was defiant.

Simon planned to attack on two fronts. One group of crusaders (it seems odd to still be calling Simon's troops crusaders, but, indeed, that is what they still were as the pope had not officially ended the crusade), led by Simon's recently knighted son Amaury, would directly assault the rebuilt fortifications. The other contingent, under Simon's direct command, crossed the Garonne on hastily constructed barges to lay siege to St-Cyprien and gain control of the two bridgeheads supplying Toulouse.

Simon had had his fill of this Toulouse, with its treacheries and deceits. His plan was based on his grandiose scheme, conjured up during his ride from Beaucaire and fed by an ego run amok, to found a "new Toulouse." After what would be his inevitable victory over Raymond VI, Simon planned to level the "old Toulouse" and build a completely new city to the west of St-Cyprien. But Simon met unexpectedly strong resistance from the unfortified St-Cyprien, and not only did the bridgeheads remained intact but Simon was unable to prevent Raymond-Roger of Foix from crossing into Toulouse with a large contingent of southern knights.

Back at the city walls, Simon's son was taking a terrific beating and losing large numbers of men to Raymond's sorties beyond the city's defenses. Simon was forced to temporarily abandon his attacks on the bridgeheads and his plans for the new Toulouse, the stone foundations of which he was in the process of laying. He reluctantly rejoined his son outside the city walls. The siege of Toulouse dragged through the winter of 1217–18. Simon and his crusaders camped in miserable tents outside the city walls or huddled in the damp dreariness of the Château Narbonnais. Raymond VI and the Toulousians, although besieged, passed the winter in relative comfort and plenty.

In December of 1217, during the deepest month of the siege, Alice was moved to action. The indomitable woman rode north through the French winter, accompanied by Bishop Folquet, to raise support for her husband. Arriving in the Île-de-France she appealed to her kin, the large and influential Montmorency family. She offered them titles to choice pieces of land in the Languedoc if they would only come to Simon's aid at Toulouse. Bishop Folquet pleaded Simon's cause directly to the king in Paris. Alice and the bishop were persuasive. Reinforcements began to arrive in Toulouse during January 1218. The following May, Alice, with Folquet still at her side, again rode south at the head of a large number of troops to aid her husband. But the growing strength of Simon's army was offset by the flood of recruits and volunteers who descended upon Toulouse from throughout the Languedoc and neighboring Aragon to serve under Raymond VI and drive out the northern invader.

After Alice's return, the pace of the siege accelerated. Simon again attacked St-Cyprien only to discover that the Toulousians had labored through the winter to dig a wide trench around the perimeter of the city that Simon's cavalry could not negotiate. Then in late May a three-day rainstorm inundated Toulouse and the surrounding countryside, making it appear that perhaps God truly *was* on Simon's side. The two bridges across the Garonne were washed away, leaving only their stone towers isolated in the swollen river. The trench that had been so painstakingly dug around St-Cyprien filled with debris and mud and could now be negotiated by Simon's mounted knights. Simon quickly took St-Cyprien and began his assault, by barge, on the remaining bridge towers. The siege was turning in Simon's favor when, in late June, a mishap at the walls of Toulouse compelled Simon to re-cross the Garonne a final time to return to his son's side. Over the miserable winter, Simon's military engineers had labored to construct a huge cat. As it was being laboriously rolled into position, a random shot from a trebuchet behind the walls of Toulouse struck the machine, severely damaging it and rendering it immovable.

On 25 June 1218, Toulousians poured out of the city gate in an attempt to destroy the cat before Simon's engineers could repair it. Simon's brother, also in the fray, was badly wounded in the struggle. Simon rushed to the scene, joining the confused mass of men fiercely fighting around the machine. The women of Toulouse continued to load and fire their trebuchets, indiscriminately raining missiles of stone and masonry onto the men of both factions. Whether ironic, preordained, or just a classic case of being in the wrong place at the wrong time, one of the pieces of heavy masonry homed in on Simon de Montfort, crushing his skull and killing him on the spot. Ten years after he first came south with the crusaders, seven years after he ordered the burning of four hundred heretics at Lavaur, and three years after his triumphal entry into the city of his desire, Simon de Montfort lay dead in the blood-reddened, trampled dirt outside the walls of Toulouse.

· THIRTEEN ·

Passing the Torches

THE PEOPLE OF TOULOUSE REJOICED WILDLY WHEN THEY heard the news of Simon's death. Church bells pealed. Women danced and sang upon the parapets and banged tambourines. Parades were organized. Amaury bore his father's body back to the Château Narbonnais. There, during the emotional night after Simon's death, Amaury de Montfort was unanimously elected to succeed his father as the secular leader of the Albigensian Crusade. After his father's death, the young Amaury was unable to gain the advantage against either Raymond VI or his son who, after having fought Simon to a standoff at Beaucaire, had returned to Toulouse and rejoined his father.

Although they were approximately the same age, the sons of Raymond VI and Simon de Montfort could not have offered a greater contrast. The future Raymond VII was smart and aggressive and every bit the same type of man his father was. Amaury, on the other hand, was neither the tactician nor the leader of men nor the frightful scourge that the Languedoc had come to expect from the de Montfort clan.

In July 1218, Amaury de Montfort raised the siege of Toulouse, abandoning the city that his father had so triumphantly entered only three years before, and retreated to the family stronghold of Carcassonne, where Simon's remains were interred in the

Cathedral of St-Étienne within the walls of the fortified Cité. Simon's death marked the beginning of a rash of defections from the rule of the de Montfort family in the Languedoc. First to go was the Agenais district in the western Languedoc. Then the town of Nîmes in the east, near Arles, recognized the suzerainty of Raymond VI as the rightful count of Toulouse and its sovereign overlord. The count of Comminges, whose territory lay to the southwest of Toulouse, soon drove the remaining northern loyalists from his lands. With the hateful Simon dead, the fear that the northern conquerors from the Île-de-France had inspired in the southern lords evaporated, as if blown away upon a fresh wind. This realliance, based upon the sudden turn of events, was a familiar formula in the Languedoc, part of its historical tradition, and once the defections began, the eighteen-year-old Amaury was unable to stanch the flow of southerners reembracing Raymond VI and the old house of Toulouse.

Pope Honorius III was consumed with the newly launched Fifth Crusade to the Holy Land, as decreed at the Lateran Council of 1215, but he did attempt to rally support for the new head of the Albigensian Crusade. The pope wrote to Philip Augustus and offered the French king half of all the taxes paid by the French clergy to Rome if he would aid the young crusader in holding the south against Raymond VI. Alice de Montmorency once more traveled to the northern courts, this time in the company of the southern bishops, to plead her son's cause much as she had on behalf of her husband.

It was neither the pope's offers nor Alice's pleas that moved Philip Augustus to action, but the king's fear that another powerful northerner would take advantage of the confused situation in the south to seize the Languedoc for himself. The king's concern lay in the person of the young Thibaut IV, the powerful count of

Champagne. Thibaut was of the same generation as Raymond VII and the young Amaury de Montfort, only eighteen years old, and already considered the personification of medieval chivalry. Not only was Thibaut judged to be both courageous and handsome, he was also the author of clever poetry and songs of courtly love, which would eventually earn him the appellation "le Chansonnier." Thibaut already possessed one of the richest regions in northern France, and he was in line to inherit the kingdom of Navarre. The French king felt it necessary to take some sort of action in the Languedoc, not for the purpose of settling the dispute between the de Montforts and the house of Toulouse, but to ensure that the Languedoc remained out of Thibaut's hands. So while Philip Augustus kept his own eye trained on England, he again dispatched his oldest son, with a large contingent of knights, to represent the interests of the king in the south.

Young Louis still had no great interest in the affairs of the Languedoc, so it was with reluctance that he set out for the south in May 1219, traveling not down the Rhône River valley, as was the custom, but taking a westerly route to the Languedoc, by way of the region of Poitou, in order to join Amaury de Montfort in the ongoing siege of the town of Marmande near Bordeaux. Louis brought with him an army sufficiently large to cause the garrison defending Marmande to surrender when he rode into sight. While the commander of the garrison and his knights were spared, the remainder of the townspeople, in an act of terror reminiscent of Béziers and the early years of the crusade, were, to a soul, slaughtered. After the bloody work at Marmande, Louis moved on to Toulouse, where he laid siege but raised it after only six weeks. His troops had served their forty days in the service of God, sufficient time to gain both the spiritual and the temporal privileges granted to crusaders by the papacy. Thibaut had been put on notice regarding the king's interests in the south. With their main goals accomplished, Louis and his army turned their backs on the Languedoc and retraced their route back to Paris.

These would be my last days in Toulouse pursuing the Albigensian Crusade and the fate of the Cathars. The events of the thirteenth century would be moving on to other places, and I would follow them to their conclusions. There were still things that I wanted to see in Toulouse, however. In the reaches of Les Jacobins that I had not yet visited was an exposition called "Les Croisades, L'Orient et L'Occident d'Urbain II à St Louis 1096–1279." At the far south end of the church was a ticket booth, and I handed over thirty francs to the two men in it. I passed through a small wooden door into the colonnaded square of the open-air cloister. The manicured gravel paths bisected the little garden with the geometric precision characteristic of French public gardens, dividing the cloister into pleasing orders of triangles and squares and rectangles.

I was the only visitor, and the sense of peace I had felt in the church heightened as I walked toward the exhibit, accompanied only by the click of my shoes on the smooth stones of the floor. Even the birds, still wheeling about, seemed muted. Along its eastern flank the cloister adjoined the charter house of Les Jacobins, along with the Chapel of St-Antonin, and the entrance to the great hall known as the refectory. All three dated from around the year 1300 and, with the cloister, achieved a subdued harmony.

Outside the refectory, in the Chapel of St-Antonin, on temporary walls erected for the exhibit, hung a large map of Europe and the Near East marked with the routes of the major crusades to the

Holy Land. Revisionist historians consider the crusades, in general, to be the first of the European colonial wars, combining cultural intolerance with abuse of power and religious fanaticism. The word *crusade* did not even come into general use until after the year 1250. Before then, these journeys ostensibly undertaken to liberate the Holy Land had been called simply voyages or expeditions or pilgrimages.

The crusaders are now generally considered to have been bloodthirsty brutes, pillaging and destroying all in their wake. Some historians, however, voice a different perspective, believing that we should not ignore or forget the initial motivation of the crusaders or the suffering they endured or their so-called *élan mystique*, the mystical spirit that drove them.

Any armed pilgrimage sanctioned by a papal bull and under the direct authority of the church in the person of a papal legate qualified as a crusade. The crusaders usually wore distinctive clothing or carried crosses and were granted the spiritual and temporal privileges guaranteed by the Church of Rome. There were eight great crusades to the Holy Land between 1096 and 1270, as well as a number of smaller crusades in the west where campaigns of extermination were carried out against heretics and other enemies of the papacy. The Albigensian Crusade certainly filled the bill as a crusade in these respects, as it did the revisionist view of the Crusades in general as wars of colonial conquest.

The actual artifacts gathered from the epoch of the crusades filled the entire length of the refectory. I scrutinized medieval prayer books carried by crusaders from Europe to the Holy Land, along with holy medals, amulets, scapulars, and coins from various realms the crusaders traversed, on foot or by horseback. I saw the enormous iron swords, crudely formed and sporting broad blades, their long handles unadorned save for a metal knob on the end to prevent them from escaping the grasp of the blood-slippery hands that wielded them. Daggers shone under glass, fully one-third as long as the swords, and simple stirrups for horsemen and something called a *masse d'armes*—a war club equipped with a spiked head. Chain mail gleamed dully and seemed fashionably modern, like a prop for a sadomasochistic music video.

Works of European art from the period lay revealed in long glass cases. The Syrian and Egyptian art on exhibit, small sculptures, metalwork, and fine glassware, revealed itself as more delicate than the European artwork, which was crude in comparison. In the rear of the refectory were several large cases given over to medieval relics and their reliquaries, the buying and selling of which was a booming business during the two centuries that the crusades flourished. The reliquaries ranged from a tiny glass phial that held, perhaps, a portion of a tooth of some minor saint to the life-sized shape of a man's shirt sleeve made from silver. From this sleeve emerged a graceful silver hand that extended upward to heaven. Visible behind a clear glass panel set in the sleeve was the right forearm of Saint Thomas—Saint Thomas the Apostle, not the medieval philosopher.

Around the final corner of the exhibit, amidst several drawings of trebuchets and other siege engines, I finally stumbled across the famous *pierre du siège,* which I'd been looking for in the Cathedral of St-Nazaire in Carcassonne. The siege stone, said to be a medieval primer and a history lesson in the conduct of siege warfare, was supposedly on loan and being exhibited somewhere in Rome, but here it was in Toulouse, on display in Les Jacobins.

The *pierre du siège* did not impress me. It was smaller than I had imagined, and battered with age. All I could make out of the worn shapes was a confusion of men, carved well out of proportion to the walls which they were either defending or attacking. Some cowered, some rode horses, others shot arrows. I moved on and found something that brought the thirteenth century alive for me. Mounted, most unobtrusively on a wall, so discreet that I almost strolled right past it, was a seven-hundred-year-old document on loan from the Archives Nationales in Paris, elegantly hand-lettered in Latin and dated 10 August 1238, relating directly to Toulouse and the Albigensian Crusade. It was a papal bull, so called because it carried the sacred seal of the pope imprinted on a *bulle de plombé*, a round, flattened piece of lead about the size of an American quarter. Apparently, the younger Raymond had at some time or another emulated his father by being excommunicated from the church, because in front of me was the official Absolution of Raymond VII, comte de Toulouse, by Pope Gregory IX.

Suddenly I envisioned the secretary to the pope laboring over the Latin prose that sprawled to the very edges of the parchment. I could hear the hooves of the horse carrying the courier dispatched from Rome with the papal bull that allowed Raymond VII to return to Christendom and reopened the gates of heaven to him. I envisioned Raymond opening his absolution with trembling hands. This small piece of parchment, crowded with writing I could not read save for the date, resonated within me and linked me tightly, almost viscerally, to those long-ago events.

I left the exhibit, returning through the cloisters, pondering the final quotation inscribed on one of the temporary walls. It was from Voltaire and went a long way toward explaining why the Albigensian Crusade, which began with the passionate fervor of a holy war, became a war shaped by greed and the goals of material conquest. "La plus grand des passions est la pillage." To pillage is the greatest of all passions. Outside the church, back in the twentieth century, the Gypsies still begged. This time I kept moving and they left me alone.

With the attention of Honorius III squarely focused on reclaiming the Holy Land, the French king embroiled in affairs across the English Channel, and with Thibaut IV, the count of Champagne, understanding that Philip Augustus would not permit his interference in the Languedoc, Amaury de Montfort was left to fend for himself against the rejuvenated house of Toulouse. Prior to the victory at Marmande, made possible by the king's son and the troops he brought with him, Amaury had sustained a telling defeat at the small town of Baziége. Both Raymond VI and his son had come to the conclusion that Amaury de Montfort was neither the warrior nor the holy terror Simon had been.

Over the next three years Amaury lost more territory; castles and towns switched allegiance to Raymond VI in a slow and grinding war of attrition. From July 1220 to March 1221 Amaury still had forces strong enough to mount a lengthy siege of the town of Castelnaudary, but Amaury's younger brother Guy was killed during the fighting. The siege proved unsuccessful, and the young de Montfort was again forced to withdraw. By 1222 Raymond VI had regained all the territory lost to Simon de Montfort since the beginning of the Albigensian Crusade in 1209, save for the city of Narbonne and the perennial stronghold of Carcassonne.

Then, suddenly and without warning, and with the total conquest of the Languedoc within his grasp, Raymond VI died. Because he had never been fully absolved by the church, even though he claimed and appeared to have been a thoroughgoing penitent,

Raymond VI was denied the sacrament of last rites and, most terrible of all, was not allowed to be put to rest in ground consecrated by the church. His body remained in a wooden coffin outside the doors of St-Sernin while Raymond VII endeavored to convince the church to lift the ban on his father. Raymond never succeeded, and his father's coffin remained on the doorstep of St-Sernin for some three hundred years. Then, one day in the 1500s, someone took note that the rotting box containing what was left of the old count had finally disappeared.

In 1223, the year following the death of Raymond VI, Raymond-Roger of Foix passed away. His son and heir, Roger Bernard of Foix, proved to be the equal of the bullying old count. Philip Augustus also died in 1223, and his son, Louis VIII, who had traveled to the Languedoc four years before, assumed the throne. They were all gone now: Pope Innocent III, Simon de Montfort, Raymond VI of Toulouse, King Philip Augustus—the generation who first ushered in the Albigensian Crusade had faded from the scene.

The fighting in the Languedoc between Amaury de Montfort and Raymond VII had dwindled to almost nothing. Amaury, exhausted from the years of struggle, with the vast majority of his lands in the south lost, with his father and brother dead, was broken, both in body and in spirit. He could no longer fight on. On 16 January 1224 Amaury de Montfort entered into a truce with Raymond VII, abandoning the Languedoc to the house of Toulouse. Amaury returned north, bearing away from Carcassonne in mournful procession the bodies of his father and brother, both of whom were finally laid to rest in the soil of the Île-de-France. As Raymond VI had been forever denied burial in sanctified ground, Simon de Montfort was denied a final resting place in his coveted Languedoc.

Raymond VII reoccupied Carcassonne and Béziers without resistance and returned them as fiefs to Raymond Trencavel, the son of the former viscount so treacherously imprisoned while under a flag of truce outside the walls of Carcassonne. The struggle in the Languedoc had, it seemed, come full circle. The Albigensian Crusade, an apparent northern victory only eight years before, even if only politically, now seemed to me an abysmal waste of time and men and a wretched, bloody failure.

My last stop in Toulouse was at the Cathedral of St-Étienne, located in a quiet square fifteen minutes from the Place du Capitole in the opposite direction from the Basilica of St-Sernin. The present cathedral had been built over four hundred years, from the beginning of the thirteenth century to the seventeenth. As I approached, I saw shrouded scaffolding erected along the cathedral's north side. The squat western portal, facing the heat of the empty Place St-Étienne and giving entry to the oldest section of the cathedral, a low vaulted nave called the naïf Raimondine was also being cleaned and restored. Garish orange construction tape kept people at a distance from the grimy, crumbling facade.

The architecture and the general impression of the cathedral can hardly be called harmonious. A small metal plaque mounted low on the stone walls a few steps within the nave attests that the construction began in the year of Our Lord 1209 by order of Raymond VI of Toulouse, as a sign of his commitment to Rome and Catholicism and to debunk his connection to the Cathars. Raymond reused parts of the old church foundation as a base for his new nave. Folquet of Marseille, the irascible bishop of Toulouse, had the final say-so on the design of the western facade that the count of Toulouse, the alleged protector of heretics, sponsored. The nontraditional exterior, two small arched alcoves to the right of the main entry set over by one large, recessed alcove, to which a traditional rose window was later added, reflected the architecture of the Iberian Peninsula—heavily influenced by the occupying Moors—rather than the French Gothic style.

The interior of the nave is spanned by a single curved vault, sixty-two feet in length, exactly as high as it is wide. The north wall is lined with dark and heavy tapestries from the sixteenth and seventeenth centuries, supposedly detailing the life of Saint Stephen. In truth, the interior of the nave was too gloomy for the tapestries to reveal much of their subject matter. Raymond VII carried on the work of his father, perhaps as part of his efforts to have the excommunication of his father lifted by the pope, contributing funds in 1249 to continue the construction of the nave.

The eastern wall of the naif Raimondine held a magnificent stained glass window designed to catch and shine the purity of the early morning light. The window contained the likenesses of three persons. In the middle was Saint Dominic; flanking him, on the right and left, respectively, were Pope Gregory IX, the absolver of Raymond VII, and Raymond VII himself. I craned my neck to have a good look at them. All three men were handsome and had far-off expressions in their eyes.

There were many stages in the construction of the Cathedral of St-Étienne. Although the naif Raimondine was the oldest part of the cathedral it wasn't destined to be the main body of the church, the building of which was begun a little to the east in 1272, a year after the city passed into the possession of the French crown. Because the old nave was supposed to be torn down, the architects did not align the old nave and the new church with much care. As a result, the nave, which was not torn down owing to a lack

of funds, wound up an offset antechurch that opens with a pronounced jog to the north into the main portion of the cathedral. It
took two hundred more years to finally finish the walls of the new
church. Lack of funds also resulted in a ceiling, not installed until
1609, that rose only 91 feet instead of the originally anticipated 121
feet. As a result, the interior seems squat, even though it rises thirty
feet higher than the vault of the old nave. The unpleasant confusion of the architectural styles make the Cathedral of St-Étienne
seem messy and unfinished. It certainly lacks the symmetry and
grace of both St-Sernin and Les Jacobins. But, then again, the
Languedoc in the thirteenth century had been in a state of confusion and change. For better or worse, it was being transformed
from a distant region of minor concern into a possession of the
king of France governed directly by the crown, the first steps in the
shaping of modern-day France.

I wandered into the main part of the cathedral, where a priest,
inaudible from the confines of the nave, was saying Mass before a
congregation of fifty to seventy-five people. I had arrived during
the consecration, when bread and wine are miraculously transformed into body and blood. The Mass was being said in French
and the congregation responded in French. When I was a child the
Mass was still said in Latin. Now, the mystical rite being conducted
before me in an unfamiliar language sparked memories from my
childhood and my Catholic upbringing. The host, in the hands of
the priest, was raised to the congregation for adoration. I felt compelled to kneel and look up at the bread in the hand of the priest,
now transformed into something other than it appeared to be.

Here was the true object of my chase—the mystery of belief.
The real Catholic Church was *here,* in what this small congregation, their eyes fixed on the host, believed in their hearts, not what
they knew from their minds. Their truth allowed them to leave

their pews and walk forward to eat of the host and enter into Holy Communion with God. At the moment that the priest raised the host in the cathedral and as the people went toward the altar, some part of me yearned to be a part of this—to believe. But in *my* heart, I knew that it was a belief I did not possess.

I couldn't bring myself to walk around the main body of the church while Mass was still going on. I left as the last of the communicants were still going forward. I considered it a strange sort of tribute to my Catholic upbringing that even a fallen-away Catholic who leaves a church before Mass is over—even as a tourist— considers himself to be sneaking out. But in the hot, sun-baked emptiness of the Place St-Étienne, out of the mystery and in the light of day, I experienced the same sensation I used to have when, as a teenager, I would leave church before the Mass was over—a surging sense of release, a feeling that my lungs were filling with fresh air, the headiness of feeling, at last and of my own will, freed.

· FOURTEEN ·

The Bridge at Avignon and the End of the Crusade

BUT WHAT OF THE CATHARS? LIKE THE THIRTEENTH-CENTURY
French Catholics who battled each other in the Languedoc, I, too,
had abandoned the chase for the Cathars and become caught up in
the political intrigue and the struggle for secular control of the
south. For all intents and purposes, beyond the grisly mass executions in the early years of the Albigensian Crusade under Simon
de Montfort, the Cathars were largely ignored. After the great
burning of heretics at Lavaur in 1211, the Cathars no longer sought
refuge in the fortified cities, abandoning them in favor of isolated
mountaintop fortresses perched above the isolated valleys of the
Pyrenees.

Twenty years of almost constant warfare had only resulted in
Cathar gatherings that were smaller and, perforce, more clandestine. The Cathar church and its hierarchy, including both the simple Believers and the Perfects, still existed in the Languedoc.
Their rituals, including the *consolamentum*, were still practiced in
the Languedoc nearly two full decades after the initial wave of
crusaders marched down the valley of the Rhône River and toward
the first great slaughter at Béziers. The simple explanation for
the persistence of the Cathars—apart from the endurance and
strength they garnered from their beliefs and from the teachings of
the Perfects—is that no one in the Languedoc throughout the long

and painful Albigensian Crusade was particularly good at identifying and catching heretics. Neither the bishops appointed by Innocent III, strong men though they were, nor the crusaders themselves were sufficiently versed in the religious orthodoxy of the Catholic Church to ferret out heretics by simply questioning them about what they believed.

It is probable that many more Catholics than Cathars were killed in the years after 1209. In any case, the Cathar Perfects, proclaimed pacifists, would rarely, if ever, have been involved in actual combat in the Languedoc. In Narbonne, for example, which had never been home to a great number of heretics, there were probably more Cathars in the city in 1229 than in 1209. Some historians credit this supposed increase, however, solely to the death, in 1227, of Arnaud Amaury, who allegedly delivered the chilling order at the walls of Béziers, "Kill them all! God will know his own."

In any case, two events conspired to refocus papal attention on the problem of the Cathars. The first was the abject failure and dissolution, in 1221, of the Fifth Crusade to rescue the Holy Land from the infidels. The second was the death, in 1223, of the French king, Philip Augustus. Seeking a salve for the bitter wound left by the failure of the Fifth Crusade, Honorius III turned his energies to the persistent thorn in the church's side, the matter of the heretics in the Languedoc. He hoped the new French king might be more amenable than his father had been to aid the pope in this matter, and so he broached the idea of remounting a crusade against the Cathars with Louis VIII early in 1224, a crusade to be led by the king himself. Honorius III tried to persuade the king that the Cathars in the Languedoc could not be allowed the freedom to spread their heresy in the lands newly reclaimed by the sons of the old southern nobles.

From the start of the talks Louis made it clear that he had certain demands that Rome would have to meet in order for him to undertake a crusade to the Languedoc. First, he insisted that the church pay all of the expenses he might accrue on such an expedition. Second, the king would follow no calendar but his own and must be allowed to come and go on the crusade as he saw fit. Finally, Louis insisted that he have the blessing of the pope to annex any lands taken by the king's army during the campaign.

Although Honorius desperately wanted the king to go south, he feared setting such a costly precedent for someone to take up the battle on behalf of Mother Church. Instead of agreeing to the king's demands, the pope countered with a proposal that Louis only display a show of force in the Languedoc, in the hopes of putting a scare into the young Raymond VII and preventing him from becoming what his father had been, a protector of the Cathars.

The king rejected the pope's suggestion out of hand and went with his army, as the old king had done so many times before, to Poitou to do battle with the English, who had recently laid new claim to the region. But the pope got what he wanted, anyway. Poitou, situated near the northwestern edge of the Languedoc, is close enough to the territories controlled by Raymond VII that he was intimidated by the might of the French king.

Raymond submitted himself to the church, as his father had done, but the cadre of southern bishops were loath to trust the count of Toulouse any more than they had his father. Raymond spent most of the year of 1224 humbling himself before the pope and the numerous church prelates in the Languedoc, but the church hierarchy remained both staunchly opposed to Raymond VII and convinced that only a strong northern French presence, a new Simon de Montfort, could preserve the rights and power of the Catholic Church in the Languedoc and put an end, forever, to the heretical threat posed by the Cathars.

In February 1225, the pope appointed a cunning cardinal named Romanus as the new papal legate to the king of France. Romanus was a son of the famous Roman house of Frangipani, praised throughout its history for great political astuteness and diplomatic prowess. Throughout 1225 the smooth and refined Romanus stayed close by the side of Louis VIII, accompanying the king whenever he traveled, gradually gaining Louis's confidence and interjecting himself into the French political arena.

On 30 November 1225, Romanus oversaw a council of the French clergy at the city of Bourges, wherein Amaury de Montfort and Raymond VII presented competing claims to the lands of Toulouse. Raymond expressed contrition, bowing to the authority of the church in all matters and swearing to do all the church would have him do, including restoring church property to the bishops and seeking out and expelling of Cathars from the Languedoc. Raymond was impressive, but with Romanus manipulating the final outcome, the decision of the council was a foregone conclusion. They ruled in favor of Amaury de Montfort and against Raymond VII.

In January 1226, Romanus wedded the desires of the Catholic Church with the expansionist ambitions of Louis VIII. Meeting with Louis and a number of other northern nobles, Romanus renewed the excommunication of the young lord, Raymond VII of Toulouse, along with those of his two most important vassals, Roger Bernard, the new count of Foix, and the young Raymond Trencavel, viscount of Béziers. Amaury de Montfort humbly ceded to Louis his family's claims on the southern lands his father had captured, after which the king proclaimed Amaury a *maréchal* of France, thus securing for him a lifelong, guaranteed income.

The groundwork was laid for Louis's entry into the Languedoc. Romanus formally entreated the king to undertake a crusade in the name of the church and drive out the heretics. Romanus offered Louis exactly the same conditions that the king had previously demanded from the pope and that Honorius III had rejected. The king was free to come and go as he pleased; he was to receive one-tenth of all ecclesiastical revenue of the French clergy for the next five years to cover the royal expenses of this undertaking. And lastly, Louis could lay royal claim to all the lands he would recover from the heretics and from Raymond VII in his role as a crusader. It was an offer that the king could not reject.

On 30 January 1226, Louis VIII formally took up the cross of the crusader. By May he had gathered a huge army at Bourges, the largest military force ever to enter the Languedoc during the Middle Ages. As this tumult of knights, mercenaries, men at arms, simple foot soldiers, and camp followers slowly made its way south along the Rhône valley, local lords rushed out to meet the king and humbly submit themselves. Representatives from the cities of Béziers, Carcassonne, Nîmes, and Beaucaire all submitted to the king en route, abandoning Raymond VII. Soon, most of the other petty nobles of the Languedoc flocked to Louis like frightened geese, honking out their loyalty to the French throne. The only city to remain steadfast in its support of Raymond VII was Toulouse, and only the count of Foix and a few other isolated southern nobles, mostly in the Pyrenees, seemed prepared to fight at Raymond's side against northern domination. Louis marched triumphantly, speeding down the east bank of the Rhône, arriving at the end of May at the gates of Avignon, a rich, powerful, and

independent city with ties to the Holy Roman Empire—and here
the king encountered his first problem, some say a problem greatly
of his own making. The king had planned to use Avignon's new
bridge, the Pont-St-Bénézet, to cross the Rhône. The citizens of
Avignon refused to let him.

The French truck drivers were again protesting the transport of
produce within their country by truckers from other countries,
mainly Spain, so I took a train to Avignon. It was a good chance to
experience a different approach to a city. The railroad station is located at the far southern end, immediately outside the walls that
still surround the core of old Avignon. The Pont-St-Bénézet is located at the far northern edge of the old town. Usually the original
streets that remain within the walls of a town built before the thirteenth century twist and turn, widen and suddenly constrict, and
follow no logic in their meandering except perhaps that imposed
by hills and rivers. But the first half of the 1.3-kilometer walk from
the train station at Avignon through the oldest quarters to the
Pont-St-Bénézet ran as straight as a shot from a crossbow.

I entered old Avignon by way of the wide Porte de la République, one of only twelve entries cut in the 4.5 kilometers of stone
ramparts that once protected the old town. Originally built in the
fourteenth century by the popes of Avignon, the ramparts must
have been even more impressive in the fourteenth century, when a
deep moat surrounded them. When the omnipresent Viollet-le-
Duc restored the walls in the nineteenth century they were ringed
by a system of boulevards, and the moat proved impossible to ex-
cavate, even for the master restorer.

The Michelin Green Guide succinctly describes the prepapal

city. "The town had existed uneventfully until, in 1309, Pope Clement V (elected Pope in 1305) took up residency there." This was at the invitation of the French king, to escape the local wars that plagued southern Italy at that time. Successive popes stayed for a century and indelibly marked the city, building palaces and ramparts and reshaping the city to their tastes. Avignon's resemblance to an early Italian Renaissance town—its architecture reminded me of Siena, especially the buildings that comprised the papal palace—was striking. As a result, the entirety of prepapal Avignon, with the exception of the Pont-St-Bénézet, is buried under the city built by the popes.

The venerable bridge, like so many medieval constructions in France, like the Abbey of St-Gilles, is given a typically miraculous origin. In 1177, a young shepherd boy named Bénézet was directed by heavenly voices to build a bridge over the Rhône at a certain point designated by an angel of the Lord. The residents of Avignon were understandably skeptical when Bénézet told his tale, until, demonstrating God's bidding, he single-handedly hoisted over his head a huge block of stone that the angel had selected for use in the bridge. After the shepherd's feat, donations flowed in. A brotherhood, the Frères Pontifes, was formed. The bridge, originally one thousand meters in length and consisting of twenty-two stone arches, spanned the river and an island that lay in its middle, and was completed by 1190, only thirteen years after Bénézet had heard his angelic voices.

The bridge remains as the last witness in Avignon to the events of the Albigensian Crusade. I needed to see it. I walked down the tree-lined rue de la République to the congenial bustle of the Place de la Horloge with its small tourist stores and cafés. Their tables were only a third full due to the hour—midmorning—and the weather; although bright and sun-filled, the air was cool and a biting breeze came off the Rhône. After I passed through the Place de la Horloge I followed a slight bend to the right, traversed a narrow, cobbled passage and entered the Place du Palais, the austere square that faces the palace of the popes. At the far end I climbed a series of stairways to gain the elaborate gardens that straddle the Rocher des Doms, the high bluff that dominates the river where the papal palace sits. Far below lay the remains of the Pont-St-Bénézet, the focal point, almost eight hundred years ago, for the unfortunate rage of a king at the head of a powerful army.

The thirteenth-century citizens of Avignon were deeply reluctant to allow the full military might of the French king within their walls, marching through their streets, and they struck upon an idea. The town would construct a temporary wooden bridge outside the city. Louis VIII and his personal escort would be welcome to cross the Rhône using the Pont-St-Bénézet. His army, however, would have to use the temporary wooden structure. Louis was furious. The king was unaccustomed to being dealt with in such a peremptory manner, especially by mere citizens. He was also fearful, and perhaps rightly so, of an ambush once he entered the city walls and was separated from the protecting bulk of his troops. Louis did not particularly want a confrontation at Avignon—it was large and well defended—but its refusal to let his troops pass over the bridge was an affront to the royal pride. In addition, there were military considerations. The Pont-St-Bénézet was the southernmost span and was both sturdy and large enough for his army to quickly cross over the Rhône. The time it would take to build the temporary bridge the Avignonese proposed would greatly delay his sweeping march to the Languedoc. Therefore,

Louis directed the legate of the crusade to denounce the entire population of Avignon as either heretics or protectors of heretics, and on 10 June 1226, he began his siege.

The king knew that a direct assault was impossible. The walls were simply too strong. However, he did have sufficient troops to patrol the Rhône and block the resupply of the city to cause food shortages. On their part, Louis's crusaders suffered horribly from a lack of adequate sanitation, and the king himself struggled with a bout of dysentery. Finally, in August, Louis mounted a full-scale assault on the town walls. The assault failed, as the king knew it probably would, but both sides experienced heavy losses. Avignon had had enough. A few days later the town capitulated to Louis. Avignon paid the king a ransom of six thousand marks, tore down its existing walls, and provided hostages as a guarantee against future trouble. Louis promised that there would be no retaliation against the citizenry, and he abstained from the systematic looting that usually accompanied a military victory. On 9 September 1226, Louis VIII and his entire army marched into Avignon. A few days later, they crossed the Pont-St-Bénézet.

From the height of the Rocher des Doms, on this clear day, with wind-driven white clouds racing along the horizon, the Pont-St-Bénézet was the perfect picture postcard of France. Beyond the profile of the slim trees that lined the bank, the four stone arches of the bridge—all that remain—extend delicately from the shore into the waters of the Rhône. Halfway to the island in the middle of the river the bridge ends abruptly, sliced clean through, as if the missing portion had been cut away by some giant swinging an ax as he trudged upstream. Between two of the remaining arches nestles the small, two-story Chapel of St-Nicolas, balanced on one of the piers. The chapel is Romanesque on the lower level and more Gothic in its upper reaches, but it is in peaceful harmony with the Pont-St-Bénézet.

The cold wind off the river had driven the other people from the exposed heights of the Rocher des Doms to the protective inner courtyards of the papal palace, and I was alone now on the rocks above the river. The wind bayed mournfully in my ears, and I heard the trampling horses with their medieval riders, the thudding boots of foot soldiers, the chanting priests, the jingling food wagons—all on the resounding march to rid the Languedoc of the heretics so many centuries ago. I climbed down the steep stairway, not toward the palace of the fourteenth-century popes, a place of grandeur and intrigues in later centuries, but to the remnants of the medieval bridge that once carried a king and his company over the muddy brown swirl of the swift-flowing Rhône.

The Pont-St-Bénézet wasn't very wide—perhaps eight foot soldiers could have marched abreast, or four mounted knights. Metal hand railings were now installed on the bridge's remaining length, and I held on to them against the strong, cold winds. The clouds hid the sun. I sought refuge in the St-Nicolas chapel. There was no glass in any of its small windows, but the stone walls sheltered me from the bite of the wind, and the chapel itself, stark and devoid of furnishings, had a peaceful aura about it.

I descended the narrow circular stairway to the lower level of the chapel. A small doorway led to a little semicircular terrace resting on one of the piers of the bridge. Here, only a few feet above the brown currents, the rush of the wind in my ears was replaced by the rumbling flow of the river. I was protected from the wind by the bridge itself. Just then a racing cloud chose to reveal the sun, which shone full strength on the little stone island. My body quickly warmed, and, as when any discomfort is removed, I felt, from head to foot, a surge of happiness. I was alone and sunshine forced an impromptu song. I hummed the tune by which every French child comes to know the Pont-St-Bénézet.

"Sur le pont d'Avignon On y danse, tous en rond . . ."

The fall of Avignon to King Louis VIII resounded through the Languedoc. More nobles rushed to surrender to him, and Louis garrisoned their towns, establishing administrative centers that would answer to him in far-off Paris. By establishing these administrative centers Louis invented governmental bureaucracy. He also consumed the entire summer of 1226—prime fighting time— and depleted the number of men he would have available for upcoming battles. But these administrative centers firmly established the lasting rule of the French king in the Languedoc.

Louis eventually reached Toulouse, but not until mid-October, too late in the season to launch an attack. The king turned north, toward Paris, but halted at the town of Montpensier in the region of the Auvergne. Louis, still suffering from the effects of dysentery, had fallen gravely ill. He died at Montpensier on 8 November 1226, as much a victim of his pride as of the illness that took him.

After the death of Louis VIII, the new king of France was the twelve-year-old Louis IX, the child king destined to be canonized as Saint Louis less than thirty years after his death at the age of fifty-six in the year 1270. Blanche of Castile, his mother and the wife of Louis VIII, was regent to the new king. Romanus Frangipani remained a close adviser to the crown. As a result of his father's success, young Louis held all the former Trencavel lands in the Languedoc—Albi, Carcassonne, Béziers, and all the lands east to Beaucaire on the Rhône. Raymond VII of Toulouse fought on for two more years against the new king's military governor in the south, a young nobleman from the north named Humbert of Beaujeu. Humbert and his force of five hundred knights, in only sporadic fighting, eventually reduced Raymond's holdings to only the city of Toulouse and a few small parcels of land north of the city.

But twenty years of near-constant combat had finally made the Languedoc weary of war. Southerners once loyal to the house of Toulouse turned their backs on Raymond and accepted the inevitability of northern rule. In November 1228, Oliver de Termes, one of the last of Raymond's loyal lieutenants, whose château had suffered terribly under Simon de Montfort's siege two decades before, defected to the king. In addition, Gregory IX, the new pope elected in the spring of 1227, when old Honorius died, had been clamoring for a full-blown renewal of the crusade.

Seeing no way out, Raymond asked for terms from the king's regent. A truce between Raymond and the forces of the crown was declared in December 1228. Peace talks began in the town of Meaux, east of Paris, to finalize the treaty and end the Albigensian Crusade. The treaty formally established the boundaries that separated the lands still controlled by Raymond VII from those won by Louis VIII three years before. The treaty also designated Raymond's daughter, Jeanne, as his sole heir (even if he were to father more children, which proved not to be the case) and gave her in marriage to Alphonse, the king's brother. All of Raymond's lands were to be the inheritance of Jeanne's children by Alphonse. If Alphonse and Jeanne were childless, all the lands of Toulouse would revert to the king.

The Treaty of Paris, as it was finally called, was ratified in that city on 12 April 1229. Raymond VII was reconciled with the church and recognized as the count of Toulouse. His penance was meted out in front of the still uncompleted Cathedral of Notre-Dame de Paris. Present to witness it were Louis IX, the young king, and the newly consecrated bishop of Narbonne, as Arnaud Amaury, the man who had witnessed the scourging of Raymond's father in St-Gilles more than twenty years before, had died in 1227. Also in the audience was the only witness to the entirety of the Albigensian Crusade, the still rambunctious Bishop Folquet of Toulouse. The French monarchy was now in an undisputed position of power in the lands that ran from Gascony to Provence and was the dominant power in the once-independent Languedoc. After twenty-one years, the Albigensian Crusade was officially concluded.

Only a few final spasms of secular revolt against northern French power occurred in the Languedoc after 1229, but they were infrequent and generally short-lived. In 1240, for instance, Raymond Trencavel raised some troops and threatened Louis IX's garrison at Carcassonne for several days. He was driven off and wisely made his peace with the king.

In September 1249, Raymond VII of Toulouse died. His holdings, as dictated by the Treaty of Paris, were inherited by his only child, Jeanne. Jeanne and Alphonse preferred to rule their lands from their house in Paris. They visited Toulouse only once, in the year 1251. Jeanne and Alphonse, childless, died in the year 1270, as did Louis IX. The lands of the former house of Toulouse passed to the new French king, Philip III. Under Philip, the Languedoc prospered during the late thirteenth century. New cathedrals were begun in Albi, Narbonne, and Carcassonne. The city of Béziers was rebuilt and repopulated. But the old Languedoc was gone forever.

The tangled lattice of lesser nobility and their courts in the

Languedoc, where the troubadours sang and played, were gone forever. The troubadours themselves were dispersed to Italy or Spain or to the north of France. Paris now ruled the south, and the culture of the north eventually enveloped the culture of the entire country. The first step that would lead to the modern French state, the France we recognize, had been taken.

The French monarchy continued to expand its domain. In 1349, France purchased outright the city of Montpellier from the king of Aragon. By the end of the fifteenth century, the territory of Provence, part of the Holy Roman Empire during the Albigensian Crusade, was absorbed into the kingdom of France. In 1658, Louis XIV, the Sun King, gained the Roussillon coast from the Spanish under the Peace of the Pyrenees treaty. France now consisted of the familiar hexagon formed by the Pyrenees, the Atlantic Ocean, the valley of the Rhine River, the western Alps, and the Mediterranean Sea.

But what of the Cathars?

FIFTEEN

The Inquisition and the End of the Heretics

HUMMING IN THE SUNSHINE ON THE WIND-SHELTERED
Pont-St-Bénézet and my refreshing love of Toulouse aside, twenty
years of chasing a war, even an eight-hundred-year old war, had
worn me out. Siege, starvation, and disease. Entire towns razed or
torched. Entire populations slaughtered—hacked to death, run
through, strangled, trampled, beheaded, or burned at the stake.
Mass mutilations. All the blood and stink of medieval combat
with its mock glory and its grisly truth.

I needed a respite from pursuing both the Cathars and the crusaders, a quiet place to put aside the horrors of the thirteenth century, a place to gather my energy before facing what would be the
last stop on my journey, an isolated, mountaintop fortress called
Montségur hidden deep in the Pyrenees where the Cathars made
their final, futile stand.

I decided to retreat to the shores of the Mediterranean, which
I had not laid eyes on since before the first slaughter at Béziers.
(I could say that I had last seen the Mediterranean six weeks ago. I
could also say I had not seen it since the unusually hot spring of
1209. Both statements were true.) This respite would be a fur-
lough, a weekend pass from the Albigensian Crusade, when I
would let the blue waters of the Med rejuvenate me.

The French truck drivers were no longer on strike; the *routiers*

had dismantled their road blocks and automobile traffic again
flowed unencumbered. I retrieved my Peugeot and headed west
and south on the Autoroute Languedocienne. The road was fast
and empty, and in three hours I was nosing through the empty
streets of the coastal resort of Argelès-Plage. Argelès-Plage marks
both a beginning and an end. It is here that the extensive string of
look-alike beaches and modern resorts of the low-lying Roussillon
coast give way to the seclusion of the Côte Vermeille. This final
twenty-one miles of French coastline before the Spanish frontier
shelters unpretentious towns, modest resorts, hardworking harbors secreted in the coves between the precipitous red cliffs and
rocky headlands that jut into the sea. Their coloring gives the
coastline its name.

The natives of the Côte Vermeille claim that their true cultural
roots are neither French nor Spanish but Catalan, born in the
eleventh century when the Côte Vermeille was part of Catalonia,
an ancient, autonomous region that hugged the arcing coast between France and Spain. The Côte Vermeille has been in the
hands of the French only since 1658, when France and Spain finally
established the modern-day border between the two countries. I
chose the Côte Vermeille because, as part of Catalonia, it had been
neutral ground during the Albigensian Crusade, siding with neither crusader nor Cathar, and had remained unpillaged territory.
I would have no thirteenth-century massacre sites to inspect, no
ruined castles to circumambulate, no stone memorials to the victims of medieval warfare to photograph, no crumbling carved
inscriptions to copy. There would be no distressing tourist attractions based on the obscene torture devices of the Inquisition. The
Côte Vermeille would be neutral ground for me, too, an opportunity to put off for a time chasing the heretics to their grim destiny.
I would immerse myself in the twentieth century.

I knew what I did not desire from the twentieth-century Côte Vermeille: the entrapping fury of the high season—still six blessed weeks away—when the streets of Argelès-Plage would boil with overheated, deodorant-failed, lobster-red tourists in the first libidinous spasms of their annual *congé* under the potent heat of the southern, high-summer sun. What I did desire was my personal vision of off-season perfection: a clean and quiet hotel, modern enough to be equipped with cable television (mindless, fingertip diversion) and private bathrooms, conveniently located near the shore's uncrowded edge. I would stroll along while the blue water played a gentle game of tag with my toes. Only infrequently would I have to sidestep the occasional frolicking child haphazardly supervised by a white-skinned, British nanny busy smoking cigarettes and flirting with some unemployed young Frenchman. I would drink beer and indulge in some common European fast food, a *croque monsieur et frites* perhaps, at a gaudy and vulgar but relatively empty seaside café. There would be a sufficient number of people to offer pleasant distraction, but not enough to crush me while waiting for a table at dinnertime.

Argelès-Plage was planned as a seaside resort and built during the 1930s. It is a true beach town: there is no real industry or business other than the tourist trade. After driving around the town, which proved to be even emptier than I supposed, I pulled up to the front of the Hôtel Plage des Pins. All of the hotels and down-at-the-heel private homes that line the sea in Argelès-Plage are no taller than four stories. All are painted white or light pink or a pastel. All project the feeling of the contented middle class.

The Hôtel Plage des Pins was a salmon color faded by exposure to ocean and sun. Still, it was a pretty place. The hotel has been owned and operated by the Xatart family since 1934, when it first opened. The current generation of owners, Pierre and Lily Xatart, had run the place since 1969. The off-season prices at the Hôtel Plage des Pins allowed me to take a corner room with a balcony that wrapped around the corner, where I could view the sea and the rugged Pyrenean foothills immediately inland.

By the time I settled into my room it was very late in the afternoon. I sat on my balcony, thoughtfully equipped with two chairs and a small white table. The slanting afternoon sun was about to retreat behind the hills, tinging the more distant of them with soft reds while those nearer the sea staunchly remained shades of green. The Mediterranean would, for a few more precious minutes, maintain its piercing and eternal blue before resolving to black. The beach held only a few souls. Perfect.

I had enough time before dinner to walk the town's newly laid, two-kilometer-long brick promenade that stretched from the hotel to a harbor dotted with pleasure boats. The promenade ran along a narrow strip between the sandy beach and the thin, narrow stand of maritime pines, from which my hotel took its name. I passed only a few other strollers. We acknowledged each other with polite, distant nods. I passed a merry-go-round that was riderless and yet emanated a repetitive but pleasant stream of music. Farther along on the promenade was an open area ambitiously named the Grand Rond, equipped with an outdoor stage. Tomorrow, there was to be an on-stage exhibition of the *sardana*, a lively Catalan folk dance performed to the accompaniment of the *cobla*, a small band composed of wind, brass, and percussion. I made a mental note to attend.

That night I was too tired to bother with the television, but fell asleep quickly to the regular rumbles of the Mediterranean coming ashore. I awoke to what I thought was the sound of waves, but they had changed since last night. They had increased in volume and were lower in pitch. My travel alarm read a few minutes past 7:00—it should have been bright outside. But beyond the balcony there had only been the slightest change in the sky, from black to dark gray. I put on my pants and stepped out.

The sunrise had been transformed into a mockery. The lower section of sky was a uniform gray that gave way to a thick, chunky gray a few hundred feet up. The sea was darker than the sky, with turbulent water white-capping and piling high in the open ocean and ungainly, sour-looking waves shuddering onto the shore. Rain plopped like cold bullets, denting the sand. The roar came not from the waves but from a giant tractor that chugged back and forth along the beach on clanking treads, pulling a huge beach rake behind it. The tractor chugged past a military-straight line of four old men who stood with their hands behind their back, respectfully marking the machine's progress. I turned my face toward where the mountains should have been. Dirty fog and thick, low clouds shrouded the mountains and dissolved the winding coastal road into the gray soup.

I descended to the breakfast room that adjoined the small lobby. It was empty save for Pierre and Lily and a young woman behind the desk. Pierre paced nervously, glancing out the window. Whenever he looked out the window, he tugged on red suspenders. A stretch of bad weather, even in the off-season, would do a resort hotel keeper no good. Pierre glanced at me, suspicion in his eyes. He was perhaps a touch superstitious and related my arrival with the onset of the foul weather. Lily's sensible face showed no concern. She had seen bad weather spring up overnight and disappear as quickly, she told me. It was nothing. They struck me as the sort of long-together couple who, over the years, have grown to be exact opposites of each other. "La mer," said the young woman behind the desk, a Xatart daughter as it turned out, "est un peu agitée." A little stirred up. I laughed at her typical French understatement.

A beach town in the rain is pathetic. The midmorning shore was empty, the four old men drying off somewhere. I climbed into the Peugeot. The streets were glistening and empty. I made my way to the Grand Rond. Rain pooled and dripped on the bare stage. A handwritten, ink-streaked sign announced that the exhibition of the *sardana* had been canceled. All the beach towns along the Côte Vermeille would be in the same shape. So I went inland, looking for diversion, to Argelès-Ville, an old town located a mile directly west of the beach town. It was Saturday, market day.

The Saturday morning market in the town of Argelès Ville spreads out from the shadow of the squat tenth-century church, a church so nondescript it was not included in the spinning rack of postcards at the town pharmacy. The market filled the church square and sent its veins down the narrow, cobbled streets that make up the oldest quarter of this old town.

The market suffered in the rain. Idle vendors stood behind long tables and wheeled carts, all of them covered with makeshift protection, beneath which heaped everything under the dripping Catalan sky: embroidered table cloths, fresh vegetables, large, rough-looking brooms, carved wooden toys, olives, ornate picture frames, neatly stacked, newly caught fish. The vendors outnumbered the shoppers. I bought two handsome peaches from a gray-haired, fine-featured man. He chose my peaches himself, sliding his hand underneath the sheet of plastic and expertly extracting them from the neat, pyramidal pile of fruits so as not to disturb the arrangement of the rest.

I returned to my hotel and sat quietly for a time in the echo of the small sitting room next to the lobby. The desk clerk (from her looks not a Xatart) was absorbed in a Maigret mystery. Pierre and Lily had disappeared. I tried watching television but the French daytime fare was even more vacuous, if possible, than its American counterpart. I ate my peaches on the covered balcony of my room. The gray-haired man at the market had chosen well. The peaches were as ripe and full of juice as they were handsome.

The day slid into late afternoon. Two solitary surfers, alone except for each other, fought the rain and wind for at least a half hour, paddling through the rough water, and finally caught the big, gray wave they had been waiting for. They rode the wave home, its final break throwing them onto the beach like rejected Jonahs. From my balcony it seemed like a warning. Don't come back out here again. But they did, paddling out, fighting the rain and the sea again, to find and ride another wave to its death upon the sand. I admired their insane persistence, laboring salmon-like against the flow of things, but I also thought them foolhardy.

I had been struggling against the current of my own thought, unable to expel the Cathars from my mind. I was reminded of the heretics everywhere: the medieval shadow cast by the old church at Argelès-Ville; the foolhardy persistence of the surfers; the trilingual (English/French/German) Gideon Bible in the top drawer of the desk in my room under the thin, local *pages jaune.*

According to Michel Roquebert, the author of the poorly edited little book I had picked up in Carcassonne regarding Cathar beliefs, there were many biblical references and compelling arguments for the righteousness of the Cathar beliefs, especially in Revelations, the last book of the New Testament.

There was this:

Then I looked, and, lo, on Mount Zion stood the Lamb
and with him a hundred and forty-four thousand . . . who

had been redeemed from the earth. It is these who have not defiled themselves with women, for they are chaste.

Or this:

And I saw the dead, great and small, standing before the throne, and books were opened. Also another book was opened, which is the book of life. And the dead were judged by what was written in the books, by what they had done . . . and if any one's name was not found written in the book of life, he was thrown into the lake of fire.

The idea of a New Jerusalem and a final judgment based upon the righteous actions of one's life as put forth in Revelations certainly seemed to give a sort of logic to the ascetic behavior of the Cathar Perfects.

The rain thudded outside. I drew my chair toward the open door to the balcony, dug the Gideon Bible out of the desk drawer, and opened to Revelations. My heretics were unshakable, even for the span of a weekend pass. They were now pursuing *me;* they would not let me alone, until I had followed them to their end.

The Treaty of Paris that formally ended the Albigensian Crusade required not only public penance for Raymond VII but also a solemn promise on his part to actively seek out and punish heretics. Raymond supplied the grand sum of fourteen thousand marks to the Catholic Church to help search out and expose heretics in the Languedoc. He also provided an additional four thousand marks, the salary for professors of theology, canon law, and the arts, for a new center of theology at Toulouse—the medieval nucleus for its modern-day university.

The exact methods to be employed to finally rid the Languedoc of the Cathars were now addressed by the new pope, Gregory IX, who had assumed the papal throne on 19 March 1227 after the death of Honorius III. Gregory was the nephew of Innocent III and had studied theology in Paris and canon law in Bologna, as his uncle had done. Although Gregory was seventy-two years of age when he ascended to the papacy, he was an energetic and intensely religious man, more than eager to confront the seemingly intractable problem of the Cathars in the Languedoc. Gregory was aware that the preceding twenty years of military action against the heretics in the Languedoc had been almost completely futile and that, in the light of the recent treaty, another military expedition against the Cathars would be impossible to raise.

Gregory became convinced that heresy in the Languedoc could only be fully and finally repressed by doing something that, as yet, had never been done. He decided to establish a special institution and to staff it with knowledgeable men whose loyalty lay solely with the pope, autonomous from local authority and answerable to Rome alone. Gregory's solution—brilliant, insidious, effective, and horrible—was one of the first blueprints on the management of the secret police of any totalitarian state, finally perfected by Joseph Stalin. The official name of Gregory's forces would be the Office of the Inquisition.

Gregory turned to the friars of the Dominican Order to staff his Inquisition. Perhaps their very name had something to do with their being chosen for this task. In Latin, it is a fierce sobriquet—*Domini canes* meant "the dogs of the Lord." Gregory had sound reasons for choosing the Dominicans. Their influence had been established in the Languedoc since early in the twelfth century when Saint Dominic, on one of his preaching missions to the Cathars, founded a nunnery in the small town of Prouille in 1207 for the sole purpose of receiving women reclaimed from Catharism. Second, the Dominicans were well trained in theology and orthodox doctrine and could readily spot the sort of deviation from the faith that a Cathar would exhibit. Last, most of the early recruits to the Dominican Order had lived in cities and were used to the ways of city life. It was in the cities of the Languedoc that the Cathars had proven the most difficult to ferret out.

At a church council held in Toulouse in November 1229, presided over by Romanus Frangipani, the architect of the treaty that ended the old crusades, a number of new techniques to be used by the Inquisition were laid out. Every Catholic over the age of fourteen would be required to swear an oath to seek out and denounce heretics. As Cathars were forbidden to swear any oaths, failure to so swear would be considered an admission of heresy. Those who were accused of heresy would not be allowed to confront their accusers. Also, a reward of one mark would be provided to anyone who aided in the capture of a heretic.

Because these new inquisitors would not be under the authority of the local bishops, the southern prelates were reluctant to accept their intrusion on what they had always considered their turf. The bishops did make some attempts to place the inquisitors under their authority. They were unsuccessful.

The Dominican inquisitors always worked in pairs. To expose a heretic, inquisitors usually questioned the accused about details of the Creation, or the nature of the Eucharistic wafer. The Inquisition was designed to work in an orderly way and inflicted its penalties in a graduated manner. First, the friars preached to those who had been secretly denounced to them as heretics. Those heretics who immediately repented and recanted were required to name every other person that they suspected was also a heretic, or those who associated with heretics. The denounced became the denouncers.

For a quick confession and the naming of names, the repentant heretic gained absolution by giving alms and performing one or two short pilgrimages to a local shrine. If simple questions failed to elicit a confession, the Dominicans exerted psychological pressure. Heretics who offered slightly more resistance before recanting had to don distinctive dress, usually with a colored cross on their backs, for a specified period. This exposed them to the same public ridicule experienced by both Jews and Saracens, who, under the edicts of the Fourth Lateran Council, had been forced to wear distinctive dress since 1215. The Inquisition could also bring charges of heresy against the dead. It was not unusual for witnesses dragged in front of the Inquisition to scour their brains for the necessary denouncement to save themselves, and to accuse people in their graves for twenty or thirty years of some heretical activity.

Heretics who recanted only upon threat of death were imprisoned, often for life, and their property forfeited to the church. Despite the sensationalism of the Inquisition torture chambers touted in Carcassonne, torture was rarely used by the Dominican inquisitors, and then only as a last resort. Those Cathars who relapsed or refused to recant their heresy were turned over to the civil authorities for execution.

It required only one Cathar to recant in order to bring down an entire congregation. A Cathar named Guillame de Sicre was a messenger and guide for the Perfects who continued their preaching duties. He led them through the darkness to their nighttime meetings with their dwindling congregations of Believers. When

Guillame recanted to the inquisitor at Carcassonne, he incrimi-
nated more than forty of his fellow Cathars.

By these methods, in the decades following the Albigensian
Crusade, the papal inquisitors developed long lists of denounced
heretics. The lists compiled by the Dominicans were carefully
guarded, cross-referenced, and cataloged. If a person's name appeared on several lists, that person became a focused target of the
inquisitors.

The death sentence signaled a double failure for the inquisitor.
Not only was a soul lost to God but valuable information was lost
to the listmakers. In this light, the Inquisition's biggest failure was
at Moissac, where, over the course of the year 1234, 210 Cathars
were delivered to the secular authorities for death at the stake.

On occasion, local governments and towns were openly hostile
to the Dominican inquisitors. Two Dominicans were thrown
down a well in the hilltop town of Cordes in 1233. The Dominican
house in Narbonne was sacked in 1234, and Dominicans were
booted out of Toulouse for a short time in 1235. But the Inquisition
had royal support from Louis IX and the monarchs who succeeded
him, and the Inquisition continued its laborious task of making
lists of heretics with alarming efficiency.

In 1246, the inquisitors of Toulouse condemned thirty-four
heretics in a single day; however, their average was a more modest
twenty-five per month. The actual number of inquisitors was
never very large, but a hardworking pair of Dominicans would,
during the span of a single year, hear a thousand cases and draw up
as many lists. By the 1240s, a little more than ten years after the end
of the Albigensian Crusade, what was left of the Cathar church in
the Languedoc was in desperate shape. The few Perfects who remained had been driven underground or had retreated to the few

seemingly unassailable mountain strongholds that the Cathars still controlled.

The simple Believers no longer could rely on easy access to a Perfect for instruction or guidance or to perform the all-important rite of reconciliation with God. The only religious services the Cathars dared to undertake outside of their strongholds were clandestine meetings in the woods and hidden by the night. Even these, as Guillame de Sicre had demonstrated, were fraught with dangers. As the work of the Inquisition ground on through the thirteenth century, the vast majority of the Cathar Perfects were finally identified, the result being the painful severing of the necessary connections between Perfects and Believers and the inevitable withering and death of the Cathar church in the Languedoc. Thus, what the swords of the army of God could not accomplish was, in the end, achieved over many decades by a small, well-trained, and dedicated group of men, always in pairs, endlessly traveling, tirelessly drawing up list after terrible list.

The giant mechanical *sanitizer* (the official name, as a brochure in my hotel room told me, for the noisy tractor and rake), the line of old men standing at parade rest, and the drumming rain were my faithful companions for all my mornings at Argelès Plage. The sanitizer began its daily run at 6:00 A.M., cruising the entire length of the seven-kilometer beach, smoothing the sand and injecting an antibacterial agent to a depth of six inches. The old men began lining up at 7:00. The rain never went away.

Nevertheless, my weekend pass had accomplished its purpose. Watching the movements of the blue-gray sea, the morning lineup, the sanitizer in its monotonous rumble, had rested me and cleared my mind for the next and final stop on my journey. Pierre looked glad when I checked out. Perhaps the sun would return. Lily was sad to see a paying customer depart. The desk clerk didn't seem to care.

SIXTEEN

Postscript at Montségur

I TRAVELED INLAND FROM THE COAST, HEADING FOR THE northern slopes of the Pyrenees to the lonely mountaintop where the Cathars made their final stand, the fortress of Montségur. In my mind I had come to call it the Last Place. The Michelin people highlighted this road, the D117, on their map with a green line, meaning that the route is considered scenic. Once the gray-green, scrub-filled flatness and the city of Perpignan were behind me, the Michelin people were correct. West of Perpignan, the land ascends through the dusty vineyards of the Corbières. The rows of vines marched up the slopes military precision on both sides of the D117, ascending as the road ascended, in a series of giant stair steps to an ever-higher plateau.

Within the first twenty miles of driving, as if in affirmation of Pierre's superstitious opinion of me, the clouds thinned, then dispersed, and the sun made a quick and brutal return. I passed through the small village of Maury, its windows shuttered against the late morning heat. West of Maury, the vineyards grew steeper and ended at the feet of craggy cliffs where the terrain became too steep for the vines, or any vegetation, to take root. The numbers of rows began to shrink as the cliffs closed in until there was only a single row of vines stubbornly lining the road. Then there were none.

As soon as the vines ended, the D117 curved to the left, narrowed to one lane, and plunged through a narrow, water-carved defile in the rocks. Twisting and turning I passed along sheer walls of stone on my left, and under overhanging rock. On my right was the rumble of fast moving water, a mountain cataract plunging in the opposite direction, toward now distant Argelès-Plage and the sea.

I continued down the narrow defile for seven kilometers. I felt I was driving into a secret world, in the shadow of overpowering, ancient rock that chilled me to the bone. Even the southern sun, able to enter the defile only in a few narrow, brilliant, smoky shafts from above, had lost its heat. The echo of the rocks and the noise of the water threw off the twentieth century. When I emerged from the gorge I was in a mountain world, deeper in the Pyrenees than I had ever traveled. The peaks of the mountains still bore cold snow. I drove the Peugeot through the deeply carved valley toward the even smaller road that, according to my map, led to Montségur.

By the early years of the 1240s the Inquisition had ravaged the ranks of the Perfects and totally disrupted the once-effective organization of the Cathar church. The Perfects were reduced to taking refuge in a few isolated mountain fortresses, strongholds of the Cathar faith that had not fallen to the crusaders of Simon de Montfort twenty years before. The greatest of these strongholds was Montségur. Montségur not only sheltered the largest number of Perfects but also held the last remnants of organization for the Cathar church. Under the cover of night Cathar Perfects still descended on steep and secret paths from Montségur, located atop a mountain shaped like a defiant balled fist, on the dangerous mission of ministering to their scattered flocks of Believers hidden in the secluded valleys.

Since the closing months of 1209 the territory surrounding Montségur had been in the firm control of Guy de Lévis, a noble companion of Simon de Montfort rewarded with these lands for his faithful service. But the fortress that sheltered the Cathars, built in 1204, had never fallen to him. Its walls had been reinforced with stone dragged up from the valley floor. A network of caves carved into the rock accommodated the swell of Cathars that sought refuge at Montségur over the years. Since the end of the Albigensian Crusade in 1229, large stores of grain and supplies donated by sympathizers had been steadily accumulating. While other Cathar strongholds had succumbed, Montségur grew stronger and remained untouched.

The stalemate drawn by Montségur against both the Inquisition and secular powers in the Languedoc might have endured a very long time, except for an event in 1242, an event that, if one has faith in the Cathars' practice of pacifism, cannot be explained very well at all. A contingent of knights descended from the fortress and made their way to the distant town of Avignonet, southeast of Toulouse. There, under the cover of darkness, the knights attacked and killed two members of the Inquisition who had, by coincidence, broken their journey for the night in Avignonet. We can only speculate as to motive. Revenge? Accident? Anger? In any event, the murders of the two papal inquisitors at Avignonet required a response. Louis IX and the pope decreed that Montségur must fall.

⚜

From the D117, the twisting road to the foot of Montségur is guarded by the industrial town of Lavelanet. I pulled into a graveled parking area next to the small stream that ran through the heart of town. Beat-up cars were parked every which way, like a freeze frame from a demolition derby. The water running in the stream was an oily, foaming purple, most likely the industrial discharge from a nearby textile factory.

Music, heavy Spanish rhythms interrupted by the urgent French slang of the disc jockey, was piped into the streets from loudspeakers mounted on the buildings. In the empty streets and squares off the main road the blaring music and hysterical talk sounded like never-ending propaganda. I imagined it continuing all day and into the empty night, echoing in the empty streets like something nightmarish from George Orwell's *1984*. I tried to escape the music in the thick-walled Romanesque church of Lavelanet. I deposited several francs into a machine to illuminate the intricately carved Renaissance organ in the choir loft, but I could not focus my mind on what my eyes saw. The hellish noise from the loudspeakers permeated even these venerable, thick walls.

The main thoroughfare, a truck route joining east and west, was under repair. The hammering and rough shouts of the men at work joined the drone of passing trucks and the noise from the loudspeakers to make Lavelanet a purgatory of noise. Besides, there appeared to be nothing of the thirteenth century remaining here that required my attention. I retreated and got out of the town as fast as I could, happy to push on to the finality that awaited me in Montségur. A few kilometers east of Lavelanet, I turned south off the D117. Once I was out of town and away from the truck route, a serene quiet reasserted itself.

Montségur is made up of two parts. There is the village, not quite a thousand souls, that rests in the valley below the mountain, and there is the abandoned fortress that occupies the heights of the mountain, a thousand feet above. I turned a final corner on the road to see them simultaneously.

The streets of the village rose in steps, following the switchbacks in the road to the base of the stubborn rocky outcropping with its ruined fortress. Neat, modest, sturdy houses of stone or smooth, whitewashed stucco lined the road. Ivy climbed their walls. Huge rose bushes dripping giant red blooms crowded the compact gardens in front of the houses. Sturdy wooden shutters stood ready to block the heat of August or the snows of December. Traditional red-tiled roofs sported television antennas or satellite dishes or both, a blend of ancient and modern. The archaeological museum, a one-room affair, exhibited no activity. The narrow lanes were empty save for two women walking slowly side by side and a lone man tending his garden in the sun and singing loudly to himself. I looked up at the dark, gray walls of the fortress of Montségur, perched on the top of its ancient mountain.

Hugh d'Arcis, a representative of the French crown in the Languedoc and the king's seneschal in Carcassonne, was given the task of taking Montségur. In May 1243, Hugh and several thousand troops laid siege to the fortress. The garrison of Montségur numbered two hundred men. They were under the command of an able military man, Pierre-Roger of Mirepoix. It soon became obvious to Hugh d'Arcis that, even with the thousands of troops at his command, he could not surround the massive mountain. Neither could he halt the stream of reinforcements joining the small garrison.

The steep terrain hid secret paths up and down the mountain that were known only to the loyal guides of Cathar. The Perfects were still able to come and go along these narrow and precipitous routes, guided by local mountaineers, to visit their congregations. The large supply of food and water laid in over the years since the Albigensian Crusade dashed Hugh's hopes of quick capitulation from the fear of starvation, a decisive factor in so many other sieges.

As news of the siege spread, Cathars from as far away as Italy sent letters and tokens of support that were regularly carried to the fortress by messengers who easily skirted Hugh's forces. The intermittent assaults and skirmishes that Hugh mounted during that first summer, although fierce, were all beaten back by the siege engines, operated mostly by women, that defended the fortress walls.

But Hugh had his orders. The French king and the pope were determined to see Montségur fall. So, therefore, was Hugh. The siege continued throughout the fall and into the first months of what promised to be a cold and bitter Pyrenean winter. In November, Hugh was reinforced by a contingent of troops led by the bishop of Albi, a man named Durande, who was not only a bishop but a military engineer with expertise in the placement of siege engines. Durande succeeded in positioning a trebuchet on the side of a tremendously steep slope near enough to the fortress to do Hugh some good.

For three months the bishop's trebuchet pounded away at the eastern fortifications of Montségur, and the first chinks in the fortress's defenses developed. The bishop's machine inflicted major damage, and the commander of the Montségur garrison, Pierre-Roger, withdrew his troops from the eastern end to save them from the constant pounding. But Pierre-Roger wasn't worried—he firmly believed that this eastern approach, a treacherous, almost sheer rock face with hardly a foothold and totally exposed to observation from Montségur, would be impossible to scale and would therefore provide its own security.

Pierre-Roger was wrong. On a moonless night in January 1224, a volunteer group of Basque mountaineers, familiar with the mountain and experienced at climbing in the darkness, managed to scale the rock face to take possession of the eastern ramparts before the alarm could be sounded. When their presence was discovered, the Basques withstood furious counterattacks mounted by Pierre-Roger, but they would not be dislodged. With the hardy Basques holding the eastern ramparts, it would only be a matter of time before more weapons and reinforcements would reach the heights of the fortress.

For more than a month rumors of imminent rescue would spread, die out, and be resurrected. Raymond VII, the Cathars within Montségur whispered, would come to their rescue. Or the Basques would finally be dislodged and thrown down the mountain. Or Hugh d'Arcis and his besiegers would simply lose interest and leave Montségur alone. But the Cathars would be granted no reprieve. Raymond VII was still away, in Rome, busily negotiating with the pope the terms of the absolution from his most recent excommunication. Pierre-Roger failed in his final, all-out attempt to eject the Basques from the eastern slope. And Hugh did not simply go away. Knowing the defeat of Montségur was now inevitable, Pierre-Roger capitulated on 2 March 1244.

I pulled into a gravel lot at the base of the mountain, really no more than a widening of the road. A sign at the foot of the path to the fortress warned that the climb up and back, not counting any time spent exploring the ruins, would take at least two hours.

Instead of starting my climb, I decided to return to the village and visit the one-room museum that occupied the ground floor of a neat whitewashed house. It was in the museum that rational science and—what?—the mysticism, legend, romance of the Cathars met head on.

The Romantic movement of the late nineteenth century had crowned Montségur with a halo, proclaiming the isolated mountaintop a "lighthouse" of Catharism. The Romantics speculated wildly about the treasure of the Cathars, supposedly buried deep within the mountain. Did they really possess the Holy Grail? The star-shaped design of the fortress surely had some symbolic meaning. Perhaps to spur, or because of, this romantic interest in Montségur, the crumbling ruins were declared a historic site by the French government in 1862. It was one of the few sites that Viollet-le-Duc did not get his hands on.

Systematic archaeological excavation did not begin atop the mountain until the late 1940s. Over the next four decades, dispassionate study of the evidence, along with a careful look at several old documents, revealed that three separate castles had stood at Montségur over the centuries. Montségur I, as the archaeologists called it, was the original fortress and had been abandoned at the dawn of the thirteenth century. In the year 1210, the Cathar bishop of Toulouse, one Guilhabert de Castres, petitioned Raymond Péreihle (one more Raymond!), a sympathetic southern nobleman, to rebuild the fortress atop the rock on behalf of the Cathars who dwelled in the region of Montségur. It was this fortress, identified as Montségur II by the archaeologists, that fell to Hugh d'Arcis in 1244. After 1244, the old fortress was completely torn down and a new fortified castle, Montségur III, was built atop the rock by Guy de Lévis. Guy left standing no traces of the walls, or of any other structures, from the two prior fortresses. The de Lévis family would maintain possession of this final castle for the next three hundred years before they abandoned it in 1510, its usefulness brought to an end by the invention of a new weapon, the cannon.

The scientific excavations had found remnants of war. Stones thrown from trebuchets littered Montségur. About half a dozen of them, ranging in size from a soccer ball to a beach ball, were arranged in a neat row under a table that displayed several medieval drawings and a model of a trebuchet.

Most of the items, though, were everyday. Their very commonness reassured me. Worn knifes. Misshapen spoons. A single spur. Battered cooking pots. The necessary detritus of life that is accidentally lost or broken and becomes buried in the dust. Wooden sewing needles. Bobbins. A metal dining plate. A child's wooden top.

I turned my attention toward two skeletons that lay side by side in a glass-covered case. They were the remains of a man and a woman. A typed notecard next to the case said the skeletons came from the mid-thirteenth century. Were these two witness to the final days of the Cathars at Montségur? They may have been killed in battle during the long year that Hugh d'Arcis laid siege. Or perhaps they died of natural causes. Were they the remains of two Cathars? The notecard did not say. Only the deaths of noblemen and their sergeants were noted at Montségur. The common man or woman met anonymous ends.

Considering the length of the siege and its extreme difficulty, the terms of surrender offered by Hugh d'Arcis to Montségur were not harsh. The garrison of Montségur, still under the command of Pierre-Roger, was allowed to depart peacefully. The fortress

would, of course, be forfeit. Only those Cathars who refused to re-
nounce their heresy would be punished. A most generous (and pe-
culiar) condition gave the inhabitants of Montségur two weeks to
organize their affairs before Hugh d'Arcis took possession of the
fortress in the name of the king of France. Throughout those two
weeks, Believers within the walls came forward, in twos and
threes, to receive the final *consolamentum.*

On 16 March, Hugh occupied the citadel. The remaining two
hundred Perfects who refused to recant were chained and taken in
carts to the valley below the castle where a pyre already burned
fiercely. A small number of them had to be thrown onto the pyre,
but, according to observers, the majority walked into the flames of
their own accord. By the end of the day they were all dead, and the
Last Place of the Cathars was no more. The fall of Montségur
ended armed resistance in the Languedoc by those southerners
who had defended the Cathars for the last half century. By the
1250s a former Cathar, Rainier Succoni, working for the Inquisition, estimated that the remaining number of Perfects in the
whole of the Languedoc was a mere 250. Nonetheless, the Inquisition did not relax its labors. The final effort to eliminate the
Cathars centered on Toulouse between the years 1308 and 1323,
when the most famous inquisitor of all, Bernard Gui, not only per-
sonally condemned 636 individuals for heresy, but also found time
to write the infamous *Manual of the Inquisition,* a detailed how-to
book that remains a staple for secret police forces to this day. The
distinction of condemning the last known Cathar Perfect, however, goes to the inquisitor of Pamiers. It was he who, by trickery,
lured William Bélibaste out of hiding in Catalonia and sent him
to the stake in 1331.

This little museum had been good for me. The Cathars, stripped of myth and romanticism, finally became ordinary and human to me. They did not possess the Holy Grail; there was no hidden treasure of the Cathars. Those who died here had only the treasure of their faith. It was something I knew I would never possess, but for the Cathars it was riches enough.

I returned to the parking lot at the foot of Montségur to begin my climb. I started up the path, which became steeper and rockier as I ascended. After twenty minutes I began to make excuses. I had on the wrong kind of shoes—they kept slipping on the black rock beneath my feet. I had begun the climb too late in the day and would have to make my descent in the failing light. I had no water for the arduous trip, and I would become dehydrated.

Finally, I told myself the truth. I no longer had a reason to make this climb. It would be long, difficult, and anticlimactic. The hilltop no longer belonged to the Cathars. The remains that stood were Catholic remains, left by the family of Guy de Lévis. I would leave the summit for the archaeologists to dig, clean, and classify. I sat down on a large rock and looked to the mountains across the valley. The shadows were stretching over them. My chase was over. It had ended in the little museum.

The first time I had laid eyes on Carcassonne—it seemed such a long time since I saw it shining in the sunlight—I had thought of myself as a sort of time traveler. After chasing the Cathars, I realized I had become someone who travels with one foot in the present and the other in the past. The dual sense of time would, I knew, be with me in all my travels. The Cathars would be with me, too, for they and I shared the kinship of disbelief. It stemmed from different sources, but it would serve to keep us bound together. I rose from my rock and went down the path. My blue Peugeot carried me out of the darkening mountains and into the world below.

Notes

1. Frederick Goldin, *Lyrics of the Troubadours and Trouvères: An Anthology and a History* (Garden City, N.Y.: Anchor/Doubleday, 1973), p. 301.

2. J. N. D. Kelly, *Oxford Dictionary of the Popes* (Oxford: Oxford University Press, 1986), p. 186.

3. Nicolas Cheetham, *Keepers of the Keys: A History of the Popes from St. Peter to John Paul II* (New York: Charles Scribner's Sons, 1983), p. 132.

4. Jonathan Sumption, *The Albigensian Crusade* (London: Faber & Faber, 1978), p. 99.

5. Ibid., p. 47.

6. Ibid., p. 48.

7. Joseph R. Strayer, *The Albigensian Crusades* (New York: Dial Press, 1971), p. 180.

8. Ibid.

9. Sumption, *The Albigensian Crusade*, p. 62.

10. Zoé Oldenbourg, *Massacre at Montségur* (New York: Pantheon, 1961), p. 147.

11. Ibid., p. 149.

12. Ibid., p. 99.

13. Ibid., p. 158.

14. Strayer, *The Albigensian Crusades*, p. 90.

15. Sumption, *The Albigensian Crusade*, p. 168.

16. Strayer, *The Albigensian Crusades*, p. 94.

17. Michael Cardinal Brown, *Thomas Aquinas: Summa Theologiae* (New York: McGraw-Hill, 1963), p. 15.

18. Ibid., p. 17.

19. Sumption, *The Albigensian Crusade*, p. 192.

Bibliography

Bentley, James. *Languedoc.* Topsfield, Mass.: Salem House, 1987.

Cheetham, Nicolas. *Keepers of the Keys: A History of the Popes from St. Peter to John Paul II.* New York: Charles Scribner's Sons, 1983.

de Rougement, Denis. *Love in the Western World.* New York: Pantheon, 1956.

Fleming, John, Hugh Honour, and Nikolaus Pevsner. *The Penguin Dictionary of Architecture,* 3d ed. Harmondsworth, England: Penguin Books, 1980.

Funck-Brentano, Fr. *The Middle Ages.* New York: MS Press, 1967.

Goldin, Frederick. *Lyrics of the Troubadours and Trouvères: An Anthology and a History.* Garden City, N.Y.: Anchor/Doubleday, 1973.

Hughes, Philip. *The Church in Crisis: A History of the General Councils, 315–1870.* Garden City, N.Y.: Hanover House, 1961.

Kelly, J. N. D. *Oxford Dictionary of the Popes.* Oxford: Oxford University Press, 1986.

Oldenbourg, Zoé. *Massacre at Montségur.* New York: Pantheon, 1961.

Ring, Trudy, ed. *International Dictionary of Historic Places,* vol. 2. Chicago: Fitzroy Dearborn, 1995.

Strayer, Joseph R. *The Albigensian Crusades.* New York: Dial Press, 1971.

Sumption, Jonathan. *The Albigensian Crusade.* London: Faber & Faber, 1978.